The

The Edge of Certainty

DILEMMAS ON THE BUDDHIST PATH

Peter Fenner

NICOLAS-HAYS, INC.
York Beach, Maine

First published in 2002 by
NICOLAS-HAYS, INC.
P. O. Box 2039
York Beach, ME 03910-2039
Distributed to the trade by
Red Wheel/Weiser, LLC
P. O. Box 612
York Beach, ME 03910-0612
www.redwheelweiser.com

Library of Congress Cataloging-in-Publication Data

Fenner, Peter G.
The edge of certainty : dilemmas on the
Buddhist path / Peter Fenner.
p. cm.
Includes bibliographical references and index.
ISBN 0-89254-035-4 (alk. paper)
1. Spiritual life--Buddhism. I. Title.
BQ5395 .F47 2002
294.3'444--dc21   2002005817

Typeset in 10.5/14 Minion
Cover art is "Self-Illumination," by Fugai (1568-1654)
Text and cover design by Kathryn Sky-Peck

PRINTED IN THE UNITED STATES OF AMERICA
BJ
09 08 07 06 05 04 03 02
8 7 6 5 4 3 2 1
The paper used in this publication meets the minimum requirements of the American
National Standard for Information Sciences-Permanence of Paper for
Printed Library Materials Z39.48-1992 (R1997).

Contents

Acknowledgments

This book explores a set of dilemmas that invariably arise when one considers the full range of philosophies and practices contained within Buddhism. While inner contradictions are obvious to anyone who surveys the breadth of Buddhist teachings, the dilemmas I focus on surface with a particular intensity for those who follow the Buddhist path. My own feeling is that these dilemmas enliven and enrich all spiritual paths. To this extent, this book is informed by my own immersion in many of the traditions I present. I have had the very good fortune to be guided on my path by many outstanding Buddhist teachers.

In particular, I thank Lama Thubten Yeshe, Lama Thubten Zopa Rinpoche, Geshe Thubten Loden, Zasep Tulku, Geshe Lhundup Sopa, Sogyal Rinpoche and Namkhai Norbu Rinpoche. I am forever indebted to their skillful guidance that, at different times, clarified my experience and confused me, but always pushed me to discover the source of balance and harmony within myself. I also wish to thank Hamish Gregor for invaluable assistance. The book has been enhanced by his editorial skills and deep understanding of Buddhist history and philosophy. I also thank Professor David Loy for his generous foreword.

Finally, I thank the staff at Nicolas-Hays for their professional support. I especially thank Betty Lundsted—her legacy in the publishing world is deeply appreciated—and Valerie Cooper for her easy attention to quality and detail.

Foreword

How can we attain something we have always had? How do we become that which we already are? If nothing is lacking now, there is no need for spiritual effort; but if we do not realize that nothing is lacking, how does that resolve our *duhkha*? To strive is to lose what we already have—already are. Yet, if there is no spiritual problem to be solved, why do we think and feel that there is one? That paradox, or dilemma, is fundamental to Buddhism and the concern of this book, the first, as far as I know, to focus on this crucial issue. In short, what is the actual relationship between practice and realization?

The Buddhist tradition developed an extraordinary variety of mind-training meditative techniques, but something else also kept breaking through: nagging, unorthodox questions about the role of such practices, about the very need for them. During the lifetime of Shakyamuni Buddha, many people became *arhats*, some after merely listening to one of his talks. After his *parinirvana*, though, fewer and fewer Buddhists seem to have awakened, despite arduous efforts. Why? Is the problem really with us and our depraved times, or—the repressed thought we hardly dare to think—is there rather something wrong with the way we have been attempting to tread the Buddhist path?

Peter Fenner approaches these questions by first summarizing the orthodox and unorthodox ways that the different Buddhist traditions have understood that path. The chapters on Theravada, Tantra, and Dzogchen are especially clear and illuminating.

Peter then shows us how the orthodox discourse of change-through-practice and the unorthodox discourse of immediacy are, in fact, dependent upon each other. We become uncomfortable as we begin to realize that he is talking about us. Our discomfort increases in the last chapters, which reveal how our understanding of Buddhism, whether orthodox or unorthodox, remains trapped within their dualism. Having demonstrated how we are impaled on the horns of that dilemma, the final chapter . . .

But no, it wouldn't do to break the suspense and give away the ending to this important book. Don't we all have to find our own, anyway?

—Professor David Loy
Bunkyo University, Japan

Introduction

An issue not commonly raised in spiritual circles is the economics of spiritual practice. Nevertheless, we might well ask how much money, time, and effort it actually costs to become enlightened. It may seem tactless or even crass to ask such a question, and that may be why we don't often ask (or at least talk about it openly). After all, the value of the teachings is said to be inestimable, and speaking in terms of cost seems to go against the absolute necessity for rigorous discipline and practice, no matter what it costs. But we may remember that spiritual seekers such as Marpa in the 11th century paid very large sums for the teachings. Marpa seems to have had rather base ideas to begin with, apparently regarding the teachings as a way to fame and fortune; but he later became a celebrated master and was one of the founders of the Tibetan Kagyud tradition. Marpa's own disciple, Milarepa, who also became a celebrated master, put staggering amounts of time and effort into obtaining the teachings. Marpa is said to have made him build great towers and then tear them down and replace the stones in the quarry, and put him through all sorts of other highly arduous trials before imparting the teachings.[1] In any case, the idea that it is crass to talk about cost appears to be an emotional construct that we project onto the idea of spiritual, for as soon as we become involved in a spiritual path, we find the hard fact is that it does cost.

It costs money. The expenses include: books, course fees, payments for retreats; travel expenses to and from retreats and other events; donations to centers, underwriting visits of leading teachers, and sponsorship of monks and nuns; tuition fees and living expenses if we study Buddhism at college or university; and perhaps repaying loans for any or all of these purposes. It's not hard to come up with figures running into tens of thousands of dollars over just a few years. And if we factor in lost-opportunity costs, the figure for long-term practitioners can easily climb considerably higher: every hour we spend sitting on a cushion or listening to a teacher is an hour we could have spent earning money. If we have a well-paid job, or the potential to get one, the revenue we lose or forego could well run into half a million dollars, or even more.

It costs time: time spent traveling to teachings, time spent meditating, time spent in reading, studying and discussion, time spent in organizing center activities. This can run into years. And it costs effort, for *Dharma* practice calls for a great deal of effort: the will power needed to stay in retreat, to stay seated on our cushion when our mind is screaming to us that we are a complete idiot for getting into all this in the first place, and that we should just stand up and walk out right now. It demands the emotional effort of engaging and integrating alien belief systems, dealing with the disapproval of relatives, friends, or colleagues, changing traditions or teachers, suppressing our anger, overcoming our fears, and coming to terms with our unfulfilled spiritual fantasies. It demands the efforts involved in making and keeping our vows and commitments and repairing them when we have broken them.

Buddhist practice is often hard and grueling.

So how can we quantify the issue? What sort of system of spiritual accounting can we apply to it? In other words, how much money should we actually spend? As much as Marpa? How much suffering and pain should we endure? As much as Milarepa? As much as the Buddha, who nearly killed himself through extreme asceticism?[2] Will spending money, time, and effort on such scales actually help?

Whatever answer we give, the idea underlying these questions is that if we're going to invest money, time, and effort, we want to maximize the return on our investment, an investment that we may see as the most important one we can ever make. And in fact, even if we would like to condemn it as coarse and materialistic, some sort of spiritual accounting is implicit in many approaches to Buddhist practice—a particular level of investment is expected to bring a particular ratio of return. Thus if we spend money, time, and effort learning one of the Buddhist canonical languages, we expect that our increased knowledge will bring increased understanding; or if we dedicate three or four years to a retreat, we expect that such a large investment will bring a correspondingly high level of spiritual profit, and perhaps also minimize later investment. It might even make us enlightened and so close the balance altogether!

· · ·

The question therefore arises, which particular approach are we going to take to the spiritual path? Speaking the language of dollars and cents, hours and days, is in the final analysis, a variation of this question. A broader form of it is simply: Does "what we are doing" have any spiritual value? This is a very serious concern—indeed, a prime concern—for practitioners of any religious, spiritual, or psychological system. In fact, it is not only a question of finding effective practices, it is also a question of determining at any point in time, whether we are best off engaging in a practice, or just experiencing life in a less strategic and goal-oriented fashion.

This question becomes particularly acute when we consider that within Buddhism many respected and illustrious masters have taught that spending even one cent, or exerting an ounce of effort, is a total and utter waste. Worse, it is actually counterproductive because it feeds a belief that realization lies out there, somewhere in the future. According to these masters, all forms of goal-oriented practice energize a belief that insight is something—an experience, a state of mind, or a connection with reality—which really can be attained.

CHANGE AND IMMEDIACY

The approaches with which we are most familiar, and which predominate the spiritual landscape of Buddhism, are built on the assumption that something is genuinely missing in our lives. This is so obvious that we would say it is our "experience." These approaches, then, offer various methodologies designed to cultivate or recover whatever it is that is missing.

The systems aligned with this approach offer wisdom, purity, freedom, bliss, and so on, be it after many lives, within this life, through attending one or more courses, or even as a result of just one meeting with a teacher. Most systems of spiritual and psychological development are of this type. They attract a following by offering "ancient" or "innovative," "easy" or "demanding," "gradual" or "rapid" methods for achieving complete fulfillment. While their methods are very different, all these systems are predicated on the need for change. In other words, they are variations on the theme "This isn't it," and that we need to be somewhere else or someone different if we are to be truly fulfilled and happy. We shall call systems of this sort "the discourse of change."

While historically the discourse of change has defined Western psychology and spirituality, a challenge to this discourse has recently arisen, and is fast gaining ground in terms of the interest and attention it is receiving from Western seekers. This alternative perspective, which is new to the West although ancient in the East, comes at things from an entirely different standpoint. Rather than assuming that our existence is fundamentally flawed, this alternative approach suggests that "This is it," that what we are experiencing right now is the state of completion we seek. According to this perspective, we have already gotten it, we are already there—there is absolutely nothing more we need to do. The fabrication and pursuit of spiritual goals are obstacles to realizing that we are already complete and fulfilled. This "discourse of immediacy," as we shall call this approach, invites us to adopt a new orientation and a new language through which to understand spirituality.

There are many, many different stories within the discourse of immediacy. Some systems and traditions teach that we are already enlightened, and that enlightenment is our natural condition, our essential nature. The only problem (which is actually an illusion rather than a real problem anyway), is that we haven't realized our enlightened condition. According to these traditions, our burdensome thoughts and conflicting emotions are really the play or manifestation of our wisdom-mind, if only we could see this. Other systems say that the search for enlightenment is a distraction because there is really no such thing as enlightenment—the here-and-now is just the here-and-now. It is just what we think it is, and it can't be any different. This is it, because it can't be anything else. According to this view, there is no "it" to get, either in the future or in the here-and-now. Thinking that "This is it" only shows that we haven't really "gotten it."

EXPLORATION

Once we have embarked upon the spiritual path and gained a little familiarity with its various twists and turns, it is perhaps natural to do a little exploration, to check out what might lie around this or that corner—perhaps there is a short cut somewhere, a path which will lead to the goal in less time or with less expenditure of effort (not to mention less money). And in recent times, many people have come to see the discourse of immediacy as just the short cut they have been looking for. Thus many spiritual seekers who have spent years cultivating beliefs and practices based on the need for change are now shopping around for a better deal, an upgrade. They are finding themselves attracted to systems like Zen, and the Tibetan Dzogchen and Mahamudra traditions, which contain powerful expressions of the discourse of immediacy. After the struggle for change, the discourse of immediacy comes like a fresh breeze, offering a seemingly higher and more authentic spiritual perspective than goal-oriented systems of practice.

Later on in this book, we shall discuss the discourses of change and immediacy and the associated forms of spiritual practice in detail. In order to set these in their proper perspective, however, we must first survey the spiritual tradition in which they are embedded. The following chapters are therefore devoted to a brief account of the essential teachings of Buddhism. It should be noted that this account is not intended to be exhaustive, for its parameters are defined by the intentions behind this book, which will become clear as we proceed. For the moment, we might define our objective as an exploration of the question, "What conclusions can we derive by pursuing the Buddhist traditions to their logical limit?"

1

The Four
Noble Truths

We begin our account of Buddhism by considering the traditional Buddhist framework for interpreting the human condition, the Four Noble Truths. We can see the importance of this framework in the fact that these four truths are said to have been fully appreciated by the Buddha only when he achieved complete enlightenment. They also formed the substance of the first discourse he gave after his enlightenment.[1]

In a certain sense, Buddhism regards the problems involved in the human condition as a curable disease. The Buddhist point of view distinguishes healing in terms of whether the aims it fulfills are temporal or transcendental. Any tool, skill, or science that makes people feel better—by removing or stimulating particular emotions, thoughts, or physical sensations—operates at a temporal level, because it responds to a conditioned need to decrease pain and increase pleasure. According to Buddhism, the pleasure/pain mechanism keeps people locked into a self-perpetuating cycle of conditioned existence, known as *samsara*. Any teaching, or medical or therapeutic intervention intended simply to improve the lived quality of people's lives, therefore, cannot move beyond the pleasure/pain mechanism, because such tools are themselves conditioned responses designed to make people "feel better."

It follows that in order to break out of the cycle of avoiding pain and seeking pleasure, and achieve a state of supraliminal equanimity, an entirely different type of medicine is required, a transcendental one. In Buddhist terms, only the high-quality medicine of spiritual psychology or *Dharma* can relieve people of the incessant need to find just the right type and level of pleasure. Although other forms of healing have their place, only the practice of *Dharma* leads to a state beyond the very possibility of suffering. This is the sense in which the *Dharma* is offered as the ultimate medicine, for it addresses the human condition as such.

The metaphor of the *Dharma* as medicine has been used throughout the history of Buddhism. Indeed, in his own lifetime the Buddha was known as the "Great Physician" because of the power of his teaching to touch and heal all forms of human suffering. It is thus entirely appropriate that in presenting the Four Noble Truths, the Buddha followed the ancient Ayurvedic diagnostic and prescriptive principles, in which a physician ascertains:

1. Whether there is a disease; and if so, its type and form.

2. The cause of the disease.

3. Whether there is a cure; and if so:

4. The nature of the cure and its application.

In the Four Noble Truths, the Buddha applies the formula thus:

1. The human condition is problematic.

2. That problem is a conditioned phenomenon—that is, it arises through specific causes and conditions.

3. The problem can therefore be remedied by

4. Eliminating its cause.

THE FIRST NOBLE TRUTH—LIFE IS PROBLEMATIC

According to the First Noble Truth, human existence is essentially problematic and unsatisfactory. This statement has often been translated as the "truth of suffering." However, the translation "suffering" is inadequate. The Sanskrit term is *duhkha*, meaning "that which is hard to bear," and in saying that life is duhkha, we mean, quite simply, that human existence is characterized by experiences we would prefer not to have. These range from extreme physical pain to unwanted thoughts.

The First Noble Truth, then, states that human existence is essentially problematic and unsatisfactory. Wherever we turn, we are either confronted by thoughts, feelings, or sensations that we would prefer not to experience, or we are separated from things we enjoy—experiences, in other words, which are hard to bear.

According to the Buddha, even experiences that we characterize as pleasant are intrinsically problematic, since worldly happiness is never lasting. Even the most uplifting experiences or pleasurable sensations are temporary. And when we sense that such valued experiences are being displaced by an experience that we value less highly, we experience a problem. Thus although Buddhism certainly acknowledges that we have pleasant experiences, it characterizes the entire human condition as problematic and unsatisfactory.

The Buddhist scriptures speak about eight types of unsatisfactory situation. These are birth, old age, illness, death, separation from things we are attached to, meeting with things we do not desire, not finding the happiness we seek, and problems associated with having a body.

Buddhist texts also talk about "three different types of problem." We will describe these briefly, for they throw further light on what Buddhists understand by the term *duhkha*. The first type of problem is obvious or blatant suffering, which includes the problems experienced in physical pain and illness, and psychological stress. These states involve a very raw and sometimes brutal experience of pain and suffering—birth, illness, and death are instances of what some texts call the "problem of pain." The second type of problem derives from the changeable and impermanent characteristic of the world: the changing nature of human experience means that happiness never lasts, and so we cannot avoid future discomfort. A third set of problems arises from the conditioned nature of human experience. The Buddha taught that the human body is so constituted that no matter how much care we take of it, at some point it causes us pain. And similarly, we can take all the care possible in terms of shielding our minds from fear, envy, concern, and so on, but at different times we have such experiences nonetheless. The very fact that we think and feel makes us prone to problems. In other words, it is the very stuff of our bodies and our thoughts to have difficulties. This type of problem is known as the "problem of extension," or the "possibility of problems."

THE SECOND NOBLE TRUTH— OUR PROBLEMS HAVE A CAUSE

The Second Noble Truth states that the problems encountered in human existence are not imponderable or mysterious, but have a readily identifiable cause. According to Buddhist teachings, the root cause of all suffering, be it physical or mental, is lack of awareness (*avidya*). Specifically, "lack of awareness" refers to the nature of one's personal identity. The problem, in a word, is egoism.

In Buddhist terms, egoism is the false attribution of independence that people make about themselves and others. People view themselves as having some independent identity that stands outside the nexus of relationships that govern the conditioned world. Once this self or sense of individual identity has been constituted, it becomes consolidated; the self is viewed as having an intrinsic existence, as existing in and of itself, apart from the language of self-characterization. Reality, that is, becomes reified.

From a Buddhist perspective, reality (that is, people and the world) is constituted in language, and whenever people lose sight of this they suffer. This does not simply mean, of course, that the use of personal pronouns such as "I," "me" and "mine" is the root of our problems. Nor is the fault to be found in attribution of characteristics to the self, such as being female, intelligent, and so on. The problem arises when people believe that they and the characterizations that they and others make about themselves exist independently of the personal and social discourse that constitutes reality. Thus, when people believe that they exist independently of language, they involve themselves in an attempt to either preserve or destroy their sense of independent or self-sufficient existence. They attempt to preserve the sense of an independent identity when they and others make favorable characterizations of who they are. They also attempt to preserve the sense of self-identity that is correlated with pleasurable experiences. In these cases, desire develops for the continuation of the self.

The Buddha observed that people also attempt to destroy the sense of self whenever they identify with personal suffering. In other words, according to Buddhism, people are prone to interpret suffering as a personal threat to their integrity and identity. In their attempt to remove suffering and block the possibility of pain, people will call into question the very value and point of existing. They will often do this by attempting to destroy what they perceive as the source of suffering, and if this is not possible, they may be prone to destroy themselves. Thus, whenever there is a belief in an independent self, there is a drive for both existence and non-existence. There is a constant dilemma between which is preferable—to exist or not to exist.

The reification of reality creates internal stresses and tensions, conflicts with the environment, as people struggle either to avoid or to capitalize on the consequences of their own existence. The act of reifying reality stimulates the movement of reactive emotions, in particular the three primary reactions of attraction, aversion, and confusion. These three primary responses in turn give rise to feelings of desire, anger, hatred, frustration, and so on. In an immediate sense, these reactive emotions produce internal stress and conflict, and lead to self-centered forms of behavior that produce illness, disease, and impoverished lifestyles. In Buddhism, the reactive emotions are referred to as poisons, because of the way they impair a balanced and accepting experience of reality.

THE THIRD NOBLE TRUTH—THERE IS A WAY OUT

The third premise of the Buddha's philosophy is that the problematic and unsatisfactory nature of human existence can be overcome.

Buddhism affirms that there is a "way out." Indeed, there would be no point whatsoever in Buddhism if it did not acknowledge this fact. However accurate its analysis of the human condition, Buddhism without the Third Noble Truth would be simply a rather gloomy account of the way things are, with no practical upshot. This premise is often presented as the "cessation of suffering": there is a state of freedom, a way of being, that is characterized by peace and freedom. This state is said to have been achieved by the Buddha in his enlightenment.

THE FOURTH NOBLE TRUTH— THE PRACTICAL UPSHOT

The Fourth Noble Truth contains the sum total of Buddhist practice—the precise means to overcome the problematic nature of existence. In other words, the Fourth Noble Truth comprises the strategy or method to attain enlightenment.

However, the nature of that method and the way in which it is applied vary quite considerably in the three great traditions of Buddhism: Theravada, Mahayana, and Tantra. These traditions can be classified in a number of ways—in terms of their history, their lineage of teachers, their scriptural adherence, and so on. For our present purposes, however, it will be useful to categorize them as "orthodox" and "unorthodox":

ORTHODOX	UNORTHODOX
Theravada	Dzogchen
Mahayana	Mahamudra
Zen	Zen
Madhyamaka	
Tantra	

The reason for listing Zen as both orthodox and unorthodox will become apparent in due course, as will the perhaps surprising description of Tantra as orthodox. In the sense in which I use the terms here, "orthodox" and "unorthodox" refer respectively to whether a tradition applies the principles of the discourse of change, or those of the discourse of immediacy. Again, the distinction will become clearer as we proceed, but for the moment, we may summarize the approaches of these traditions as follows:

ORTHODOX	UNORTHODOX
Effort	No effort
Change	No change
Later	Now
Practice	No practice

The following chapters discuss the three traditions and their respective approaches to the Fourth Noble Truth in detail.

2

The Theravada—
Ethics and Mindfulness

Theravada[1] Buddhism represents the orthodox tradition par excellence. The teachings of Theravada Buddhism are found in the scriptures of the Pali Canon,[2] the earliest extant Buddhist texts, and Theravada claims to represent the original "insight" teachings of the Buddha.

Whatever the validity of that claim, the Theravada does convey the core doctrines and practices of Buddhism, in the sense that its teachings are accepted as foundational by the Mahayana and Vajrayana traditions. Thus, in describing the basic framework of Theravada, we are also detailing a set of understandings and practices shared by other Buddhist traditions.

Theravada Buddhism gives primary focus to laying out a path for achieving personal freedom from suffering. The state of transcending the possibility and fact of suffering is called *nirvana*. A person who achieves this state is called an *arhat*, one who has, in the words of the Pali text, "lived the life, done what was to be done, laid down the burden, gained the true goal, who has completely destroyed the fetter of becoming, and is liberated by supreme insight . . ."[3]

THE PATH OF RENUNCIATION

The Theravada path is based on a strong moral foundation of renouncing psychologically dysfunctional behaviors. Lay Buddhists are advised to follow the five precepts, which stipulate the avoidance of:

1. Taking life and harming living beings

2. Stealing

3. Sexual misconduct

4. Lying

5. Taking intoxicants

Each of these is described in some detail in the traditional texts and their commentaries, but for the present purposes it is not necessary to dwell on these details.

A considerably larger body of rules is imposed upon Theravada monks,[4] who in many ways are regarded as exemplifying the Path of Renunciation in its most rigorous form. Again, we need not concern ourselves with the details, for our focus here is the purpose behind these constraints and the perspective from which they derive. The aim of these rules, then, is to filter out all thoughts and emotions that block or dilute a direct, unmediated experience of reality—the modification of physical behavior leads to the minimizing of emotional reactions. This provides a platform on which to skillfully cultivate an experience of mental settlement and clarity.

The path of renunciation is based on the recognition that feelings of anger, fear, attraction, jealousy, and so on—what in Buddhism are known as *kleshas*, or "reactive emotions"—are a hindrance to the development of inner serenity (*shamatha*) and mental integration (*samadhi*), and that such feelings and emotions are at least partially conditioned by our physical, verbal, and mental actions.

The assumptions made on the path of renunciation are that physical behavior, emotions, and thoughts influence each other in a feedback relationship; and that by modifying any one of these, we can influence the others. It is clear, in other words, that if we change our way of thinking, we can change how we act in the world. And modifying the way we act will produce changes in how we feel and think. While our physical actions, emotions, and thoughts are all interdependent, this path focuses on removing intrusive thoughts and disturbing emotions by changing our external behavior. This can be represented as a simple formula:

PHYSICAL BEHAVIOR → EMOTIONS → THOUGHTS

In accordance with this thinking, the five precepts—and, to a far greater extent, the vows of the monk—regulate physical and verbal behavior.

According to Buddhism, the actions renounced through upholding the ethical precepts are nearly always contaminated, because they are based on either desire or aversion, which, as we have seen, lie at the very root of the human problem. As a rule, people who habitually kill, steal, lie, and so forth are not at peace with themselves. In fact, the circumstances in which harming others, dishonesty, and so on don't produce some level of ongoing disturbance are extremely rare. Consequently, if one avoids these actions, one has gone a long way toward removing the mental turmoil and inner conflict that disturb deep contemplation.

These behavioral guidelines are rediscovered by all meditators as they attempt to empty their minds of imagery, thoughts, and disturbing feelings. When meditators first sit down to cultivate tranquility, concentration, or insight, they find an almost constant stream of mental activity whose origins lie in thoughts, feelings, and actions that occurred some time earlier. For the most part, our present thoughts and feelings are residues from past experiences. Thus, in the course of a single meditation session, meditators might find themselves dwelling on a recent indiscretion they have committed, gloating over a "significant" conquest or achievement, churning with anger about how someone has behaved toward them, reliving a childhood trauma, or just wishing that they were doing something they recall enjoying.

If the experiences that precipitated these disturbances hadn't occurred, meditators wouldn't be burdened with the memories and fantasies that displace an experience of mental peace and clarity. Although one can't go back and erase the original action, it is possible to take care of one's future meditative experiences by ensuring that one refrains from contaminating actions, now and in the future.[5] Also, as one develops one's powers of concentration, one can suppress the arising of memories and images.

The path based on renouncing contaminated actions allows contemplatives to pacify their minds so that they can bring about a cessation of egocentric thoughts and feelings. Traditionally, monks work their way through a series of meditative absorptions known as *jhanas.* A passage in the Pali canon gives the Buddha's description of these sublime states of consciousness:

> [A] monk, detached from all sense-desires, detached from unwholesome mental states, enters and remains in the first jhana, which is with thinking, and pondering, born of detachment, filled with delight and happiness. And with the subsiding of thinking and pondering, by gaining inner tranquillity and oneness of mind, he enters and remains in the second jhana, which is without thinking and pondering, born of concentration, filled with delight and happiness. Again, with the fading of delight, remaining imperturbable, mindful and clearly aware, he . . . enters and remains in the third jhana. Again, having given up pleasure and pain, and with the disappearance of former gladness and sadness, he enters and remains in the fourth jhana, which is beyond pleasure and pain, and purified by equanimity and mindfulness.[6]

After lifetimes of dedicated practice in entering and leaving these refined and subtle meditative states at will, practitioners transcend all residues from earlier actions that have been contaminated by egoism, and enter nirvana, having suppressed or destroyed all traces of ignorance and egoism.

MINDFULNESS MEDITATION

The most important method in Theravada Buddhism, outside of ethical behavior, is the practice of a particular form of contemplation called "mindfulness meditation" (*satipatthana*). Seemingly a very simple practice, mindfulness meditation is in fact one of the best tools we can use on the ego, which, as noted earlier, lies at the root of all human suffering.

This method has become popular in the West, where it is taught as "mindfulness" or "insight meditation" by Western and Asian teachers such as Joseph Goldstein, Ayya Khema, and Thich Nhat Hanh.[7] In this meditative practice, we learn to recognize and observe the individual components that comprise the full range of human experience. The exercise is to attend to the different processes and phenomena that occur in the here-and-now as we are sitting in meditative posture, or engaged in the various activities of our lives. This involves systematically observing our experience to find out what is there. The process of attending to our experience is assisted by applying simple and generic labels to the phenomena we observe. Thus, when any type of sensation arises, whether auditory, visual, or any other, we simply label it as "sensation" and do not take the analysis any further—there is no need to describe what sort of sensation it is or where it comes from. In mindfulness meditation, we aren't looking for an answer to any problem we might have posed. Nor do we attend to our experience for the purpose of producing a theory or explanation about why things behave in the way they do. We simply attend to our experience.

The *Discourse on Mindfulness*[8] in the Pali Canon describes this science of observation, laying out the processes and phenomena toward which the meditator directs his or her attention. For example, with respect to one's body, one may attend to one's breathing and to the position of one's body—whether it is upright, settled, or prostrate. Within these positions, one observes whether one is looking toward or away from something, whether one is moving or stationary, bending, stretching, eating, drinking, chewing, savoring, falling asleep, waking up, speaking, or remaining silent. With respect to one's feelings, one identifies whether what one is feeling is pleasant, painful, or neither pleasant nor painful, and whether the feelings are of a worldly or spiritual nature. One also observes the arising and dissolution of these various feelings. With respect to emotions and mental states, one recognizes the presence or absence of different moods and emotions such as desire, hate, excitement, anger, worry, joy, love, agitation, torpor, and doubt. One also observes the presence or absence of ignorance, and whether one's mental state is contracted or expanded, inferior or superior, concentrated or unconcentrated, free or constrained. With respect to the different dimensions of experience (*skandha*) one observes whether one is attending to a physical form (*rupa*), a feeling (*vedana*), a perception (*samjna*), a drive or impulse (*samskara*), or consciousness itself (*chitta*). (These five items, as we shall see shortly, are of crucial importance in Buddhist analysis.) In the domain of spiritual experiences, one observes the presence or absence of mindfulness, inquiry, energy, joy, relaxation, concentration, and equanimity.

The initial task in mindfulness meditation is to see things "as they are" in order to filter out the thoughts, feelings, attitudes, and so forth, that disturb the emergence of peaceful awareness. As Ayya Khema explains:

> When thoughts arise, look at them, give them a name. Whether it's a correct label or not doesn't matter. Any label during meditation means the thought needs to be dropped. When you have learned to label in meditation, you will be able to label thought as wholesome, profitable, skillful or otherwise in daily living also. When you know it's not skillful or wholesome you can let go of it.[9]

The ultimate aim of mindfulness meditation is to bring us into contact with the raw sensory information of our experience. When we penetrate beneath the interpretative filters that analyze and complicate our experience, we discover that all phenomena are impermanent, lacking any defining characteristics, and without a self or solid core. This recognition doesn't come through looking for these characteristics. They aren't confirmed as the conclusion of an empirical hypothesis. Rather, reality simply reveals itself as constantly changing and without any abiding essence.

As this practice matures, the meditator also realizes that there is no self within the aggregation of components that constitute a person and his or her experience. There is no stable observer observing what is being observed—the very instant an observer is identified, it is seen to have the characteristics of that which is being observed. Once we turn the focus of this meditation on ourselves, in other words, we see that we share the qualities of all phenomena: we ourselves are impermanent, lacking in defining characteristics, and devoid of any solid core.

This theory is found in the earliest Buddhist traditions, which propose the doctrine of "no-self" (*anatman*). According to this doctrine, analysis discloses that a human is composed of five components and five only, known as the five *skandhas* or "dimensions of experience," which I noted previously: physical form, feeling, perception, drives or impulses, and consciousness. Even the most cherished and seemingly distinctive features of our humanity—affection, loyalty, memory, talent, aesthetic discernment—resolve into the interplay of these components. Since each of these components is impermanent and lacking in any defining characteristic, it inevitably follows that the whole that they compose must share those characteristics—it must, in other words, be *anatman*, "no self."

Nevertheless, at some level, there is a witnessing or registration of experience, but this registration dissolves into nothing as it is instantaneously replaced by another gestalt of sense data. There is no core entity linking experience together as "our" experience. Our sense of personal continuity breaks down into an experience of disparate mental constructs built on notions of time, space, and experience. We discover that there is nothing within the physical body, feelings, perceptions, drives, and mental events that constitutes a person, self, or soul.

This realization progressively frees the meditator from pain and suffering as he or she realizes that there is no self to suffer. Ultimately, the meditator ceases to exist as an independent entity. His or her conditioned experience transforms into an experience of unconditional freedom, transcending all notions of time, space, and existence.

3

The Mahayana— Compassion and Insight

Although Mahayana Buddhism in some ways represents a departure from the earliest traditions, it remains thoroughly within the orthodox framework.

Historians and Mahayana Buddhists themselves offer differing accounts of the origin of the Mahayana tradition—or "traditions," as it would be more accurate to say. Whereas Theravada Buddhism is a more or less homogeneous body of teachings, the Mahayana embraces a very wide range of philosophies and praxes, including the Prajnaparamita school, the Buddha-nature school, Pure Land, Ch'an or Zen, Mahamudra, Sahajayana, Madhyamaka, and Yogachara, to mention only a few. While these traditions all point in the same direction of awakening (*bodhi*), they differ radically in their articulation of the path.[1]

According to Mahayana Buddhism itself, the Mahayana teachings were given—or at least endorsed in one way or another—by the Buddha himself, and they represent an expansion of the earlier teachings, a more profound version suited to people of more subtle spiritual understanding. According to historians, on the other hand, the Mahayana came into prominence in Northern India around 100 B. C. E. some 400 years after the Buddha's death, as a reaction to the restraint and exclusivity of monastic Buddhism, and also as a product of universalizing tendencies within the Indian culture of that time.

For our present purposes, however, more important is the spiritual orientation displayed by the Mahayana. Whereas the Theravada is said to lead the practitioner to his or her own personal liberation, the Mahayana radically expands the horizons of spiritual practice to embrace the liberation of all life-forms whatsoever throughout the entire universe. Forsaking the goal of an isolated nirvana disconnected from social reality, the Mahayana Buddhist seeks to liberate all living creatures from the painful cycle of rebirth and attachment. The spiritual ideal of the Mahayana is therefore not the *arhat* of the Theravada tradition but the *bodhisattva*, an individual who vows to strive tirelessly for the enlightenment of all beings. Thus the *Prajnaparamita Sutra*, one of the core texts of Mahayana Buddhism, compares the bodhisattva path to the objectives of the earlier teachings, or "vehicle of the Disciples":

> [A] Bodhisattva should not train in the same way in which persons belonging to the vehicle of the Disciples . . . are trained. How then are [persons belonging to the vehicle of the Disciples] trained? They make up their minds that "one single self we shall tame, one single self we shall pacify, one single self we shall lead to final Nirvana." Thus they undertake exercises which are intended to bring about wholesome roots for the sake of taming themselves, pacifying themselves, leading themselves to Nirvana. A Bodhisattva should certainly not in such a way train himself. On the contrary, he should train himself thus: "My own self I will place in Suchness, and, so that all the world might be helped, I will place all beings into Suchness, and I will lead to Nirvana the whole immeasurable world of beings."[2]

This view of the spiritual path is inescapable in terms of Buddhism's own logic: if the self is a misleading linguistic construct, then the notion that there is a single self to lead to nirvana is an even more pernicious notion and can only be counterproductive.

The bodhisattva's motivation is thus compassion; or more strictly speaking, *bodhichitta*, which may be translated as "the urge to work for the liberation of all beings." To the bodhisattva, this urge becomes the underpinning of all action. Confronted by the reality of the human predicament, the bodhisattva is overwhelmed by an intense desire to work for the resolution of that predicament, to assist all beings in attaining realization.

It should not be imagined that the ideal of compassion is absent from Theravada Buddhism—many of the Pali texts speak of the cardinal importance of compassion. However, it is in the Mahayana that compassion receives its fullest emphasis as the quickest and most direct remedy to all unvirtuous states of mind. As the Mahayana poet-saint Shantideva says:

Whatever joy there is in this world
All comes from desiring others to be happy.
And whatever suffering there is in this world
All comes from desiring myself to be happy.[3]

Undaunted by the magnitude of their task, Mahayana Buddhists vow to do whatever it takes to free everyone from the self-perpetuating cycle of *samsara*, and dedicate themselves to upholding the Four Great Vows of the Bodhisattva:

However innumerable beings are, I vow to save them;
However inexhaustible the passions are, I vow to
    extinguish them;
However immeasurable the Dharmas are, I vow to
    master them;
However incomparable the Buddha-truth is, I vow to
    attain it.[4]

In keeping these vows, they set about acquiring all the resources needed to be of maximum benefit to everyone. In order to do this, they need to expand their capacity to communicate simultaneously with multitudes of beings, creating individually tailored learning experiences that free people from the ignorance and delusion that cause their suffering. Bodhisattvas also need to transcend their own suffering as quickly as possible, because it would otherwise limit and distract them from giving full and objective attention to the suffering of others. Thus, the twin objectives for bodhisattvas are the cultivation of wisdom (*prajna*), which ensures their own freedom; and the cultivation of compassion, which guarantees that they will never deviate from their commitment to liberate all creatures from conditioned existence.

The twin objectives of wisdom and universal compassion must be cultivated simultaneously, because only by cultivating the wisdom that sees the unreality of all existence can bodhisattvas engage the world without being overwhelmed and paralyzed by the infinite suffering they encounter. Getting the balance right in the synchronized practice of wisdom and compassion is a delicate matter for bodhisattvas—the topic is discussed at length in the playful and often intricately paradoxical dialogues of the Perfect Wisdom (*Prajnaparamita*) teachings. If they give premature or excessive emphasis to the perfection of wisdom there is the chance that bodhisattvas will become insensitive to people's suffering, because deep down they know that it is just a fabricated construction. The *Vimalakirtinirdesha-sutra*,[5] for example, warns that without compassion, bodhisattvas will gravitate toward an experience of quietism that will alienate them from other creatures. On the other hand, if they focus too much on developing an automatic impulse to become involved in the confused and painful constructions of deluded creatures, and so ignore the development of wisdom, they will find themselves consumed by the overpowering intensity of samsaric suffering. The pre-eminent skill of bodhisattvas lies in their capacity to see the utter unreality of pleasure and pain, without allowing this insight to disempower their capacity to actively alleviate the illusory suffering of the world.

In particular, bodhisattvas cultivate universal compassion, which sees other creatures' pain and confusion as needing the same urgent relief that we seek from our own suffering. In order to cultivate this outlook, Mahayana practitioners apply two sets of practices known as "equalizing and exchanging self and others," and "the sevenfold causation." Briefly, the practice of equalizing and exchanging self and others consists of realizing that all beings are, as Dickens put it, our "fellow passengers to the grave." All have essentially the same experience of the human predicament, all are as anxious as we are to avoid suffering, and so all should be treated with the same consideration that we apply to ourselves; and ultimately, their liberation from samsara should be a matter demanding the same unremitting vigor as our own.

The sevenfold causation practice consists of making an active attempt to regard all beings as our mother and cultivate toward them the same love and compassion that we feel for our mother. This practice can be linked to the Buddhist teachings of reincarnation, of course. If, as Buddhism teaches, all beings have been wandering in samsara for endless eons, taking birth over and over again, then it follows that at one time or another, all beings must have been our mother. Whether or not one is prepared to accept this reasoning, this practice is based on sound psychology. Our mother gives birth to us, feeds us, raises us, makes sacrifices for us, and undergoes many hardships on our behalf, and it is natural that we should feel enormous gratitude to her. Equally, it is natural that when we contemplate her experiencing pain, misfortune or disease, old age and death, we will be full of compassion toward her and will seek to help her, with the greatest urgency and to the utmost of our ability. If we cultivate that same attitude to all beings, then we will not hesitate for a moment to relieve their suffering and increase their happiness wherever and whenever we can; and, in particular, we will do whatever we can to assist them in transcending suffering altogether.

With this spirit of unshakeable altruism, it becomes unthinkable that bodhisattvas could hesitate, for even an instant, in turning away from actions that harm other creatures, or disturb their own clarity of perception. The magnitude of their commitment entirely displaces any thoughts of malice and all insensitivity.

In order to fully equip themselves for the momentous task of assisting other creatures to overcome their ignorance and suffering, bodhisattvas cultivate the "six perfecting disciplines" (*paramita*) of generosity, ethics, patience, enthusiasm, meditation, and insight, to which we shall turn shortly.[6]

• • •

The sheer scope of the cosmic vision of the Mahayana produced an explosion of texts, philosophical frameworks, meditative methods and institutional structures, because it was deemed necessary to adapt the teachings to the make-up and needs of a widely diverse range of people. According to the Mahayana, men, women, lay people, monks, nuns, hermits, politicians, artisans, and intellectuals—people of every type—have different needs, interests, and aptitudes, and the teachings therefore need to be customized for each user. The historical challenge for Mahayana Buddhism was to adapt the teachings to the needs of different communities without compromising their liberating power.

The Mahayana thus does not consist of a single body of teachings, and therefore does not lend itself to the treatment applied in the previous chapter to the practices of Theravada Buddhism. In the following sections, we shall therefore focus on the overall shape of Indian Mahayana, and examine a uniquely Chinese expression of Mahayana—the Ch'an or Zen tradition. Indian Mahayana is significant for our purposes for the precision with which it lays out a graduated path to full enlightenment, while Ch'an is important not only in itself but also in its popularity among Western practitioners.

INDIAN MAHAYANA

Although the Mahayana emerged into the public domain in response to the exclusivity and doctrinal conservatism of the Pali traditions of Buddhism, within a few centuries Indian Mahayana itself had grown into a solidly institutionalized and monastically based tradition, relying heavily on the traditions of textual commentary which had been elaborated in the Buddhist monastic universities. In the fifth century C. E., the greatest of these, Nalanda, was established near Rajagriha in Northern India by the ruling Gupta dynasty. In the course of the following centuries, numerous other universities were founded, notably Valabhi, Vikramashila, and Odantapuri. These seats of learning were the most prestigious in Asia, and taught both Buddhist and non-Buddhist subjects. They survived until the 12th century, when the invading Hun king Mihiragula, and later the Turks (Bakhtiar), destroyed them.

Nalanda and the other monastic universities produced a continuous stream of spiritual and intellectual geniuses, who combined the sharpest of intellects with the deepest states of meditative contemplation. The list of names reads like a "Who's Who of Indian Buddhism," and includes such luminaries as Aryadeva, Asanga, Vasubandhu, Vimalamitra, Chandrakirti, Shantideva, Santarakshita, Haribhadra, Kamalashila, Atisha, and Naropa. The works of these and other masters continue to be an invaluable source of guidance to practitioners and scholars.[7]

Each institution had its "gate professors," often the most illustrious of the teachers, who were charged with maintaining the highest possible entry standards. The great saint-scholar Naropa, for example, was one of the gate professors at the university of Vikramashila. Those who sought admission were lodged in guest houses so that the gate professors could place their personality, behavior, and intellect under scrutiny. In the peak academies, only one candidate in five was selected, after a screening process that could last several weeks. In this way, the universities attracted the brightest minds to the practice of contemplation and self-transformation.

More than universities, these institutions were virtual factories for producing realized masters, the best of whom were shipped abroad to propagate the universal mission of Mahayana Buddhism. At different times, the graduates of these universities were invited to Sri Lanka, China, Tibet, Java, and Korea in order to supervise the work of translating Mahayana Buddhism into foreign cultures.[8]

Whereas today the brightest minds are often attracted to disciplines such as medicine and science, the intellectual giants of medieval India were almost invariably drawn to the unique combination of self-reflective inquiry and contemplative practice provided by the spiritual universities. And in true scientific spirit, they applied their powers of discernment and analysis to understanding and describing the transformation of their own minds as they practiced the contemplative techniques of Mahayana Buddhism.

In doing so, they discovered that the path traversed en route to the full awakening of buddhahood is determined both by the model of practice that propels the evolutionary process, and by the structure of consciousness itself. While each person has a somewhat different experience of spiritual evolution, there are certain regularities to the process. Furthermore, as people progress on the path, they tend to identify less and less with their personal history, and so the regularities become increasingly consistent. Based on these insights, the philosopher-saints were able to trace the contours of the path to full awakening with astonishing rigor and precision. Their research produced several scientific accounts of the Mahayana path and created a new set of texts focused exclusively on the "Structure of the Path."

While the signposts and distinctions on the Mahayana path are at places arbitrary, there are certain nodes in the transformation of consciousness that lock in place a broad set of parameters shared by most Mahayana accounts of the path to full awakening. These are "mission critical events," as it were, which are determined by the structure of consciousness itself.

According to these accounts, the Mahayana practitioner, or bodhisattva, travels on a path that can be defined in terms of five stages and ten levels.[9] The five stages traversed by bodhisattvas begin with the "path of accumulation." This path is characterized by the development of the "aspiration to awakening" and the accumulation of positive spiritual energy and an initial introduction to wisdom practices. (We will return to the practice of wisdom shortly.)

As the practitioner develops proficiency in meditations on serenity and insight, the path of accumulation transforms into the "path of application." This path culminates not gradually but in a unique breakthrough in which bodhisattvas gain their first direct experience of openness. They are able to see things as they really are, without the dualistic fixation of subject and object. Previously, their experiences of openness were tainted by projected expectations of what the experience would be like, but now they have a direct, non-conceptual awareness. Qualitatively this is identical to the buddhas' insight into reality. The difference, however, is that it is short-lived.

This event is called the "path of seeing" and leads directly into the "path of meditation."

Having directly tasted the buddha mind, bodhisattvas now embark on the long journey of deepening and prolonging their awakening. The magnitude of this task can be gauged from the fact that it is said to take eons to nurture the initial breakthrough into the full awakening of buddhahood. At the beginning of this path, bodhisattvas can only access the experience of openness in the controlled circumstances of their meditation practice. When they rise from their meditation, or encounter some disturbance within their formal practice, they lose the experience. Evolution on this path is defined in terms of the capacity to stabilize and progressively extend the experience into the more challenging situations encountered in interaction with the world.

The path of meditation contains the ten stages, and a specific perfecting discipline is correlated with each stage. Thus, bodhisattvas sequentially emphasize generosity, ethics, patience, enthusiasm, meditation, and insight. These stages deal with the increasingly subtle levels of conceptual confusion, while continuing to accumulate the spiritual energy and wisdom that are necessary to amass all the awakened qualities of buddhahood. At the conclusion of this path, the bodhisattva enters the "path of no more learning." This final path, as the name implies, signifies a point beyond which nothing more is possible in terms of an individual's spiritual evolution.

The Mahayana path focuses on purifying the mind of the emotions and delusions that have perpetuated our suffering over countless lifetimes. According to the Mahayana, there are two types of obstructions to the full awakening of buddhahood. These are the "emotional obscurations" and the "cognitive coverings." The emotional obscurations produce the suffering that we experience individually. The cognitive coverings, on the other hand, create the myopic vision that restricts our knowledge and perception to the locus of our embodiment. As these coverings are lifted, the bodhisattvas' awareness expands beyond the limitations of the brain and physical senses. As they progress through the upper levels of the path, they become aware of their own and others' past and future lives; other people's thoughts are as obvious to them as their own, and they can perceive events at a distance. When all the coverings have been removed, they achieve the full awakening of buddhahood and live in the realization that their consciousness pervades the entire universe.

The perfecting discipline of wisdom is based on two distinct but complimentary techniques, known as "serenity" (*shamatha*) and "insight" (*vipashyana*) meditation, which are intimately related. Although there is a sequential dimension to the cultivation of serenity and insight, each contributes to the development of the other. (This is known in the literature as "union of serenity and insight.") In general terms, the practice of serenity precedes the practice of insight meditation. The aim of serenity meditation is to increase concentration and produce a high degree of inner settlement. Through this practice, meditators are able to be with themselves— with their own minds—for days and weeks on end without needing to escape their inner experience. The practice of serenity also brings coherence to their stream of thought and feelings so that their attention is no longer prone to the fragmentation that characterizes an untrained person's stream of consciousness. This is referred to as "one-pointed concentration of the mind." The ability to stabilize the mind is gradually developed through successive stages of meditative absorption, which produce an experience of increased physical and mental pliancy. Through these practices, meditators are able to keep their minds focused on any phenomenon they choose to contemplate, without any scattering or dilution of intention.

However, in and of itself, serenity meditation is insufficient to break through the captivating nature of conditioned existence. It lacks the power to penetrate through to the ultimate, unconditioned reality. Thus, serenity needs to be complemented with a form of meditation that is able to realize the utter insubstantiality of constructed reality. In Mahayana, the pre-eminent form of meditation for generating insight into the open and relative texture of all reality is provided by the deconstructive contemplations developed by the Madhyamaka tradition.

MADHYAMAKA—
DECONSTRUCTING FIXATIONS

Many Indian and Western philosophers consider Buddhist Madhyamaka to be the most rigorous and intellectually honest philosophical system in existence, seeing it as philosophy—as the undogmatic and unbridled pursuit of wisdom—in its purest form.

At a philosophical level, Madhyamaka can't be neatly categorized as either an orthodox or an unorthodox tradition. In fact, within the gradual versus sudden debate, which somewhat parallels the issues we are engaging in this book, Madhyamaka has been appropriated by both camps. However, for our present purposes, it falls under the rubric of "orthodox," insofar as it constitutes the application of a method with the expectation that it will give rise to a result.

The Madhyamaka system probably was developed during the fourth century C. E., by the South Indian philosopher-saint, Nagarjuna, who is considered by many Buddhists to be the second Buddha. According to some traditions, his birth was predicted by the Buddha himself. Nagarjuna's stature within Buddhism can be gauged by the fact that he is a central lineage-holder or patriarch in nearly every significant tradition of Mahayana Buddhism, including Ch'an, Pure Land, and the Tantric traditions.

According to Buddhist histories, Nagarjuna single-handedly brought the Perfect Wisdom teaching of Mahayana into the public arena. The legend goes that he was approached by a team of *nagas*, or subterranean spirits, who appeared in human form after one of his lectures at Nalanda University. These beings invited him into another space-time reality, where the Mahayana wisdom transmission was being preserved until the time was ripe for its introduction into the spiritual communities of North India. Nagarjuna spent the equivalent of fifty Earth years imbibing these teachings, and returned with a cache of priceless Mahayana texts. Having realized the full import of all these teachings, he then synthesized their intention and developed a methodology that could systematically and reliably disclose the open and essenceless nature of reality.

Nagarjuna called his philosophical crystallization of the Perfect Wisdom transmission Madhyamaka. The word *madhyamaka* means "central" or "middle-most," and the name is applied to this system of thought because it reveals an experiential space that is free of all limiting conceptualization.[10] In particular, it rigorously avoids our habitual inclination to think in terms of things being real or unreal, meaningful or meaningless, significant or insignificant. It doesn't matter whether we are talking about conditioned realities such as a personal identity and the dynamics of karmic conditioning, or the unconditioned space of openness (*shunyata*)—according to Nagarjuna, we miss the mark every time we affirm or deny the existence of these realities: reality-as-such cannot be captured through the lenses of existence and non-existence. In fact, reality cannot be conceptually captured at all, because it doesn't exist as a thing—or even as a non-thing. In the space of openness, not one single ounce of effort is expended in trying to appropriate or deny whatever is happening in the ongoing flux of existence.

In Nagarjuna's hands, Madhyamaka is pure method. It isn't a positional system.[11] It offers a cognitively based technique for dismantling any and all fixations. This is accomplished by deconstructing the conceptual bases that give rise to the attachment and aversion that cause all suffering. The precision and unrelenting rigor with which Nagarjuna was able to undermine the presumed coherence of people's belief systems gave him a watertight technology for releasing all forms of attachment and defensiveness. Nagarjuna's time in the naga realm seems to have totally rewired him! If anyone dared present him with any "truth," he would dismantle it on the spot, offering in its place a completely non-referential experience of openness.

Nagarjuna's focus was on the structures that his fellow Buddhists had become defensive about and attached to, but the generic structure of his deconstructive technology means that it can be applied when and wherever we encounter a fixed position. His texts offer a set of templates that can dismantle every conceivable type of fixation—past, present, and future.

Deconstructive Meditation

The deconstructive analyses that were laid out by Nagarjuna act as templates for one of the most rigorous forms of meditative practice found within all of Buddhism. With this method, Nagarjuna brought contemplative practice to a new level of exactness. The form of spiritual practice he developed has subsequently been refined by generations of Indian and Tibetan meditators into a streamlined and powerful method for gaining non-conceptual realizations of openness (*shunyata*).[12] In fact, according to most Madhyamaka meditators, the direct realization of openness can only be gained through this form of meditation.[13]

The aim of deconstructive meditation is to reverse the tendency of the thought process to automatically fragment and perpetuate itself. This is achieved by systematically deconstructing the commonsense belief that all things, ourselves included, have a real or intrinsic existence. The great seventh-century Indian Madhyamaka philosopher Chandrakirti writes:

> [The belief that] things intrinsically exist produces a constant stream of conceptualization. But a thorough analysis shows that nothing is intrinsically existent. [When we realize that] nothing exists intrinsically, the process of conceptualization cannot occur, just as there can be no fire without fuel. Ordinary people are limited by their conceptualizations, but practitioners become liberated through the non-conceptual [realization of reality]. The learned have said that the reversal of conceptualization comes as a result of [deconstructive] analysis.[14]

This form of meditation assumes that more can be done to de-energize the stream of interpretations that filter a direct engagement with reality than detachedly observing the flux of our experience. According to Madhyamaka meditators, the path leading to the perfection of wisdom can be dramatically shortened by using meditations that directly impact the capacity for thought to perpetuate itself.

This particular form of practice performs an "inside job" in which thought is used to bring about its own destruction. The gradual breaking down of reactive emotions and rigid ways of thinking results in a progressive induction of the insight into openness. This insight exposes the open texture of reality, wherein nothing has a substantial or autonomous existence. It is an experience in which nothing exists in-and-of-itself—everything is seen to be co-existent and interdependent with everything else.

Deconstructive meditation structurally manipulates cognition according to strict logical guidelines applied within a state of deep and concentrated meditation. Thus, when Madhyamaka practitioners meditate on openness, for example, they first develop their concentration so that they can focus their thoughts in a firm, precise, and sustained manner. Hence, they begin by developing serenity and mental integration, which we touched on earlier. These practices stabilize their emotions, and bring a new level of coherence and stability to previously fragmented and diffused thought processes. If these deconstructive meditations are performed diligently and with sufficient precision and intentionality, they thoroughly dissolve all conceptual fragmentation (*prapancha*), thereby leaving the mind of the meditator clear and spacious. This form of practice is also called "unfindability analysis," because it logically leads to the conclusion that what we thought existed, doesn't exist at all. If, for example, we are investigating the reality of our personal identity, the analysis will reveal our own non-self-existence.

The Diamond Cutter Routine

Tibetan monastics, perhaps most notably those of the Gelug[15] school, are particularly keen on these methods. In their meditation manuals, they present a "super-charged" version, known as the "Diamond Cutter," so called because, like a diamond-tipped auger, it progressively grinds away the false belief that we have an autonomous and independent existence. The internal mechanics of the Diamond Cutter method are similar to those of the Zen koan, which we will describe in the following section. The main difference is that the Diamond Cutter gradually chips away at the ego, whereas the koan intensifies the ego's search for solid grounding, bringing the dilemma of existence to a head, before a cataclysmic explosion in which the ego is destroyed in a *satori* experience. The Diamond Cutter routine offers a controlled way of producing the paradoxes in consciousness, which break down the heavy stream of conceptuality that habitually filters a direct experience of reality.

The Diamond Cutter routine proceeds through four steps. The first step establishes the analytical principles upon which a contemplative investigation is based. Here the meditator determines what is to be negated, or, in less technical language, makes a decision about what is going to be investigated. This involves distinguishing an object—such as the self—and then determining that this is the object to be analyzed, and nothing else. The practitioner makes a firm commitment about the defining characteristics of the object in question, and agrees not to reconsider this definition once the investigation is under way, since the post-hoc introduction of ambiguity would only serve to dilute the contemplation. Thus, if a meditator is investigating the reality of her or his own existence, she or he will take a firm fix on what, for the purposes of any particular meditation, will be regarded as the self. She or he may decide to focus on a set of feelings, or memories, or ambitions, or physical appearance, or all of these and any other aspects of what she or he considers her- or himself to be. But once that profile is established, it will remain in place through to the completion of the contemplation.

The second step is called "ascertaining the pervasion." Here the meditator selects a contrasting relationship through which to analyze the object selected in the first step. Thus, the meditator commits her- or himself to the principle which says that two mutually excluding alternatives exhaust all the ways in which something can exist. In other words, if something exists, then it is either A or not-A. If the object is our mind, for example, it is either physical or non-physical. If it can be shown to be neither physical nor non-physical, then it doesn't exist at all, because "being physical" and "being non-physical" exhaust all the possible ways in which the mind could exist. If the meditator is seeking to develop insight into the open nature of his or her own person, for example, then he or she will usually look at the experience of selfhood in relationship to his or her psycho-physical organism—what we will call the "body-mind." The contrasting relationship usually chosen when investigating the reality of our own existence is that we (the self) are either the same as our body-mind, or different from our body-mind.

Steps one and two are locked in place in order to reduce any slippage in the contemplation. They are designed to ensure that no residual perception of intrinsic existence is left over at the completion of a meditation.

The third and fourth steps investigate the coherence of these two options. A logical paradox is then generated for each of these alternatives.[16] The overall conclusion that Madhyamaka meditators reach is that they are neither the same nor different from, their body-minds.

At this point, Madhyamaka meditators are left with nowhere else to go in terms of finding a foundation or fixed point of reference for their own sense of separate existence. By bringing all their intellectual muscle to these contemplations, they are able to effect what is called an "analytical cessation" upon their stream of thought and gain a space-like experience of openness that is free of any limiting construction.[17]

The Destructuring of Conceptuality

The process of deconstructive meditation can be thought of figuratively as a series of steps that logically induce contradictory beliefs to coalesce at a common spatial and temporal location. As Shohei Ichimura writes: "The predicament created by this dialectic is due to the unexpected contradiction which our convention implies, and this feature is suddenly disclosed by the particular context in which two contrary entities are juxtaposed over the same sphere and moment of illumination."[18]

Deconstructive meditation forces two contradicting beliefs to be held in consciousness at the same time. However, because these

beliefs negate each other, each deconstructs or dissolves the other—
the two beliefs collapse into and destroy each other:

$$A \rightarrow \leftarrow NOT\ A$$

The meditator directly sees that reality is boxed in and cut up purely
as a function of conceptual designation. In the absence of conceptual splitting, supposedly independently existing things return to a
ground of being that cannot be said to be either dual or non-dual.

Although Madhyamaka meditation requires effort and application to counteract the energy and momentum of conceptual splitting, such splitting is viewed as an artificial condition, maintained
only through the constant investment of effort. At root, it is propelled by the need to secure our own solid and independent existence. When that effort is relaxed, conceptuality tends to naturally
fold in on itself and dissipate. According to Madhyamaka, openness
is a natural, effortless, and primordial condition of existence,
whereas conceptual proliferation is characterized by the continual
expenditure of effort and struggle (*duhkha*). Thus, for
Madhyamaka, conceptual bifurcation is the source of our suffering
in the whirlpool of cyclic existence.

Madhyamaka meditators hone and refine their contemplations
so that their conceptual trajectories, defined by their analytical procedures, become more controlled, penetrating, and focused. In this
way, they are able to produce a predictable and consistent reversal of
conceptual fragmentation. Through repeated meditations over
thousands and thousands of hours, they progressively and thoroughly eliminate all traces of the belief that they are unique and
self-existent.

ZEN—THE CONTEMPLATIVE TRADITION

In China, Mahayana Buddhism proliferated into many schools and
numerous hybrid developments. The main schools were the Vinaya
(Lu-tsung), Three Treatises (San-lun), Idealist (Fa-hsiang), Tantric
(Mi-tsung or Chen-yen), Flow Adornment (Hua-yen), White Lotus
(T'ien-t'ai or Fa-hua), Pure Land (Ching t'u) and Ch'an. Some of

the schools were highly experimental. Many were relatively short lived, while others survive in various schools practiced in Korea, Japan, and elsewhere.

Of these, the Ch'an or Zen School of Buddhism is perhaps the finest and most enduring creation of the Chinese and Indian minds. The word Ch'an itself is the Chinese transliteration of the Sanskrit term *dhyana*, "contemplation" or "meditation," and Zen is the Japanese form of the same word. While this tradition traces its origins to the historical Buddha, its roots go deep into pre-Buddhist Chinese history.[19]

As we indicated in the Introduction, Zen displays elements of both the orthodox and unorthodox perspectives. For the moment, however, we are concerned chiefly with the orthodox features of the tradition.

The official history of Chinese Ch'an begins with Bodhidharma, a semi-legendary south Indian master who is said to have traveled to China in 520 C. E. The emperor, Liang Wu Ti, was a keen patron of Buddhism and had some interest in Buddhist philosophy, so when he heard that Bodhidharma had arrived in the country, he invited him to the court and tried to engage him in discussion. If the emperor had any hopes of a stimulating intellectual exchange, however, these were speedily dashed. Mindful of his standing in terms of spiritual accounting, he asked Bodhidharma how much merit he would have chalked up from all the charitable work he had undertaken—the schools and hospitals he had built, the Buddhist texts he had had printed for free distribution, the monasteries he had founded, the alms he had given, and so on. "None whatever," Bodhidharma replied. This did not entirely please the emperor, but he asked a number of other questions, to all of which Bodhidharma's answers were equally unsatisfactory and uniformly cryptic. Finally, the emperor asked, "What is the first principle of the Dharma?" "Vast emptiness," said Bodhidharma. "And if this is so, who is it that is speaking to me?" "I do not know." The Emperor, now completely exasperated, banished Bodhidharma across the border.[20] Bodhidharma spent the next nine years sitting in front of a wall, meditating until his legs withered away. When asked what he was doing, he answered that he was "listening to the sound of the ants walking."

The next major figure in Zen history (or legend, for the two are often hard to distinguish) is Bodhidharma's disciple, Hui-ko. One day, Hui-ko approached Bodhidharma as he sat in meditation and asked for teachings, but Bodhidharma ignored him. Hui-ko repeatedly asked for teachings, but Bodhidharma refused to take any notice of him. Hui-ko had heard of the great hardships that the disciple must undergo in order to receive teachings from a master, so he cut off his left arm and offered it to Bodhidharma. Bodhidharma now decided there might be some reason to listen. "What do you want?" he asked—one imagines Bodhidharma's tone was somewhat abrasive. "I've been trying to pacify my mind for a very long time," Hui-ko answered, "but without success. Please tell me how it's done." "Bring me your mind," said Bodhidharma, "and I'll pacify it for you." Hui-ko replied, "I've been looking for my mind all these years, but I can't find it." "There you are," Bodhidharma answered, "I've pacified it." At these words, Hui-ko attained enlightenment.[21]

The third major figure in Ch'an is Hui-neng (638–713 C. E.), the Sixth Patriarch. Like Bodhidharma, there is so much legend surrounding Hui-neng that very little can be said about him with any confidence. However, it is to Hui-neng's verse encapsulating the teachings of the *Dharma* that Ch'an's identity can ultimately be traced.

The story goes that Hui-neng, an illiterate peasant, was a lay associate at the monastery of the Fifth Patriarch, Hung-jen, where he was employed as a rice-grinder. One day, Hung-jen, now an old man, decided that the time had come to choose his successor, and so he declared that he would appoint anyone in the monastery who could show a total understanding of the *Dharma*. One of the monks thus composed the following verse:

The body is like the Bodhi-tree,
The mind is like a clear mirror.
At all times we must strive to polish it,
And must not let the dust collect.[22]

Hui-neng read this verse and responded:

> *Bodhi originally has no tree.*
> *The mirror also has no stand.*
> *From the beginning not a thing is.*
> *Where is there room for dust?*[23]

We shall come later to the significance of these verses, and in particular their application in the unorthodox framework.

In the centuries following Hui-neng's enlightenment, Ch'an consolidated into two schools, the Lin-chi, which developed the practice of working with *koans* or "insight puzzles," and the Ts'ao-tung, which encouraged the practice of "just sitting" without attachment to thought or no-thought. I will discuss these practices later in this chapter.

•   •   •

In contrast to the Indian spiritual mentality, the Chinese seems to be pragmatic. Where the Indians delight in complex metaphysics, the Chinese appreciate the practical and immediate rewards that come from balancing the needs of the mind and emotions, self and other, openness and structure. Thus in Ch'an we see a return to the very essence of the Buddhist "middle path."

In the centuries following the Buddha's death, monks and scholars in India and elsewhere sought to formalize and codify the Buddha's teaching. Driven by the need to understand the full import of the founder's wisdom, they developed complex and sophisticated analyses of the path to enlightenment, which they explained in very considerable detail in erudite philosophical treatises and commentaries to the scriptures—in this connection, we have already noted the output of the great Indian Buddhist universities. However, from the Ch'an point of view, philosophical investigation and analysis are futile, since enlightenment is ultimately not knowable—it can only be experienced through the radical deconstruction of dualistic states of consciousness. The aim of Ch'an, therefore, is to create conditions that replicate the mind-state of the

Buddha when he sat under the bodhi tree in the lead-up to his full awakening.

Ch'an's praxis is thus designed to break down the dichotomy between the sacred and the profane, and to integrate the activities of contemplation and daily life. Ch'an cautions practitioners against becoming attached either to inner quietude or to external activities; and even after their enlightenment experience, Ch'an practitioners seek out meaty situations to test and deepen the quality of their realization.

It wasn't until the close of the 12th century that Ch'an was introduced to Japan. In 1191, Eisai brought the Lin-chi tradition of Ch'an to Japan, where it is known as Rinzai; and in 1244 Dogen introduced the Ts'ao-tung form, which became known as Soto. Rinzai Zen (we shall henceforth use the Japanese forms) found most of its adherents among the cultured elite, who were attracted to the forceful koan method, designed to bring about a sudden awakening called *satori*. Soto Zen, which favored a more serene and contemplative approach, initially spread through a lower social level. Both traditions remain very vital in Japan today (and, indeed, in the West).[24]

·   ·   ·

Since enlightenment is unknowable, words are useless both in describing it and in attaining it, and so Zen literature abounds with tales of how Zen masters have conveyed their teaching nonverbally. Thus, for example, when the sixth-century master Fu Ta-shih was asked to give a lecture on a certain Buddhist sutra, he climbed on to the platform, struck the lectern with his staff, and then climbed down again.[25]

Although it is found in other Buddhist traditions also, the hallmark of Zen is "sudden enlightenment," where realization is attained from one moment to the next. Sometimes this occurs in association with some trivial incident, and sometimes through a crisis provoked by the master, whose insight enables him to choose exactly the moment when the student is ready to be zapped, as it were, into insight:

Hyakujo ... one day went out attending his master Baso.... A flock of wild geese was seen flying, and Baso asked:
"What are they?"
"They are wild geese, sir."
"Whither are they flying?"
"They have flown away, sir."
Baso, abruptly taking hold of Hyakujo's nose, gave it a twist. Overcome with pain, Hyakujo cried aloud, "Oh! Oh!"
"You say they have flown away," Baso said, "but all the time they have been here since the very beginning."
This made Hyakujo's back wet with sweat. He had satori.[26]

Zen revels in the paradoxical nature of the spiritual path, and is totally upfront in teaching that there is nothing whatever to learn. Many Zen insight riddles and teaching stories explicitly or implicitly illustrate this approach. The following is a typical example:

A monk said to Joshu, "I have just entered this monastery. Please teach me."
"Have you eaten your rice porridge?" said Joshu.
"Yes, I have," said the monk.
"Then you had better wash your bowl," said Joshu.
With this, the monk gained insight.[27]

The message here is that preoccupation with goal-oriented systems of practice entirely misses the point. When you've finished dinner, just wash the dishes—there isn't anything else to be done, and it is an illusion to imagine that there is. The mirror is already clean, as Hui-neng pointed out, and so there is no need to polish it. There is no mystery lurking behind reality waiting to be revealed, and therefore there is no special practice that will reveal it. This is "it," and there isn't any more.

Simply Sitting (Zazen)

The tradition of mindfulness meditation is also central to Zen Buddhism, in which it is variously known as *zazen* ("sitting meditation") and *shiken taza* ("simply sitting"). In Soto Zen, mindfulness practice takes the form of simply sitting. In his great work the *Shobogenzo*, Dogen claims that "Zazen is not the means to enlightenment, zazen itself is the completed action of the Buddha. Zazen itself is pure, natural enlightenment."[28] He describes zazen thus:

> To practice zazen choose a quiet place that is neither drafty nor damp, and use a thick mat. . . .
>
> The place for zazen should not be too dark but kept moderately bright day and night. It should be kept warm in winter and cool in summer. Keep the body and mind at rest—cut off all mental activity. Do not think about time or circumstances, nor cling to good or bad thoughts. Zazen is not self-consciousness or self-contemplation. Never try to become a Buddha. Detach yourself from the notions of lying or sitting. Eat and drink moderately. Do not waste time. . . .
>
> Do not sit on the middle of the cushion but place the front part under your buttocks. Cross your legs and put them on the mat. The cushion should be touching the base of your spine. This is the basic posture that has been handed down from Buddha to Buddha, Patriarch to Patriarch.
>
> Use either the full or half lotus posture. In the full lotus, the right foot is placed on the left thigh and the left foot on the right thigh. Keep your legs horizontal, and your back perfectly straight. In the half lotus the left foot is placed on the right thigh and the right foot is tucked underneath the left thigh. . . .
>
> Loosen your robe and straighten up. Right hand on left foot, left hand on right foot. The thumbs should be straight and touching lightly. . . . Remember to keep your back straight at all times. . . . The eyes should be kept open in their natural way. . . .[29]

There seem to be two ways to stimulate an intense observation of the ego. One way is to remove all structure and meaning from living, so that there is neither reason for doing what we are doing, nor any way of determining whether we are on or off track in terms of our spiritual aspirations. In this situation, the ego constantly searches for grounding and reference by creating its own systems of meaning in order to have a purpose and to track its performance and progress. The other way to stimulate the ego's defenses is to impose a severe level of constancy and uniformity on one's physical activity. In this case, the ego tries to break out and affirm its own uniqueness and independence against a background of discipline imposed from outside. Zen chooses the latter method.

Although there has been a perception that Zen endorses a "let-your-hair-hang-down" approach to spiritual practice, nothing could be further from the truth—in fact, its level of physical regulation is strict in the extreme. There is no question of being able to let your hair or anything else hang down, even outside the highly regimented meditation sessions that Zen employs, since the discipline extends far beyond formal sitting practice. Every aspect of one's waking and sleeping life is dictated by highly formalized ways of acting. When one arises, how one sleeps, how one washes oneself, how one cleans one's teeth—all are regulated. How one walks and talks, and even how one eats—all are regimented. There are no opportunities to "do your own thing." There is no such thing as your own interpretation of the rules and procedures. The culture of Zen monasteries is to flatten or level the ego—hence no one takes any personal interest in one's breakthroughs or disappointments. This extreme level of regimentation is designed to drive the ego crazy as it attempts to express its difference. This brings the ego into high profile so that the student can observe its need to maintain its own uniqueness and existence.

The main difference between mindfulness meditation and simply sitting is that in the latter, less texture is laid over our experience. Whereas in mindfulness practice we are offered a set of predefined categories through which to observe our experience—labels such as "sensation"—in simply sitting, the practice is to be aware of our thoughts, feelings, and physical sensations as they naturally present themselves to us. We don't even distinguish between our thoughts, feelings, and so forth unless this is what we are already doing. In simply sitting, one enters a state "without thinking."[30] This is not a state of not-thinking, for this would exclude thoughts. Nor is it a state of thinking, for this would preclude no-thought. So, in simply sitting, we enter a disclosive space that allows whatever is there—thought or no thought—to be there, just as it is.

Insight Puzzles (Koans)

In the Rinzai school of Zen, the practice of simply sitting is combined with the use of koans, or "insight riddles."[31] The koan method of practice began in China in the 12th century with Sung masters, and was systematized in Japan in the 13th century. In the course of time, a large corpus of koans was produced, and some masters prefer to draw on these, while others evolve fresh koans as circumstances suggest.

The koan is a kind of puzzle or problem, a conundrum that defies conceptual resolution. A master gives a student a koan with the intention of bringing to the surface a fundamental dilemma that lies within the student's mind and which obscures spiritual awakening. Sometimes the koans are dialectical in structure—for example, they might report a terse exchange between a famous master and a student. A well-known koan of this type comes from an exchange in which a monk asked the ninth-century Chinese master Chao-chou (Japanese: Joshu), "Has a dog Buddha-nature or not?" Chao-chou answered: "*Mu!*"[32] In time, this developed into the koan, "Show me mu!"

This koan and its background are multilayered, even if approached conceptually. *Mu* literally means "no," so at one level Chao-chou seems to be saying that a dog does not have the buddha nature. However, it is fundamental to the Mahayana traditions, including Zen, that all beings possess the buddha nature. If taken literally, Chao-chou's answer is thus profoundly shocking in conventional Buddhist terms—if we imagine a Christian priest denying the divinity of Christ, we will get something of the flavor. Clearly, then, there is something else going on—the answer is not to be taken literally. In fact, *mu* also stands for emptiness, the open-ended dimension of being, so at another level, Chao-chou is referring to that realization which lies beyond the dichotomy of subject and object. The question whether a dog has the buddha-nature is posed by the dualizing mind, and so any answer acceptable to that mind will necessarily operate in terms of the dichotomy of subject and object. But from the perspective of shunyata, such a question becomes altogether futile, and all the terms and assumptions that the question uses become irrelevant.

Thus the challenge, "Show me *mu!*" ultimately means, "Show me your experiential understanding of the open-endedness of being." And there is no way this understanding can be demonstrated conceptually. Hence, the answer to this or any other koan does not take the form of a reasoned analysis or a statement of Buddhist doctrine. There is, in fact, no way of pre-determining a "correct" answer to a koan. And indeed, there is no such thing as a single correct answer. The student might give a solution in a statement as seemingly nonsensical as the koan itself, or in body language, or even in silence, but the master will know whether the answer demonstrates that the student has solved the koan—whether, that is, the answer comes from the awakening mind.

Koans such as *mu* have a tangential bearing on Buddhist doctrine, although Buddhist doctrine will not assist one whit in their solution. Other koans are nonsensical utterances or questions. Hui-neng, the Sixth Patriarch of Zen, often set his students to work on the koan, "What was your original face before your mother and father were born?"[33] And Hakuin Zenji, a great reformer of Rinzai Zen, used to ask his students: "What is the sound of one hand clapping?" Alternatively, a master might deliver the koan to a student by holding up a staff and saying: "This is not a staff. What is it?"

Koan practice, then, is driven by the need to find a solution to a problem that is intractable in conceptual terms, and to present that solution in non-conceptual terms. By working through a series of koans, the student progressively dismantles the cognitive structures in her or his psyche that give rise to personal and spiritual conflicts. If this process is handled skillfully and diligently, the student will have a non-conceptual insight experience (*satori* or *kensho*), which is a taste of the full-blown experience of illumination or enlightenment. This experience, which is undeniable and revolutionary in its nature, then takes progressive hold in the student's life as it is assimilated and consolidated. The first experience of insight is expected within two or three years of beginning koan practice. The full integration of this experience could take another ten to fifteen years.[34]

It is difficult to underestimate the intensity of the process leading up to the first experience of satori. D.T. Suzuki likens the process to being asked by the Zen master to climb to the top of a hundred foot pole and then "execute a desperate leap utterly disregarding your existential safety."[35] The leap, of course, is the transcendence of egocentricity.

The initial objective of the koan is to propel the student into an experience called the "great doubt." The immense effort that the student has expended in working on the koan comes back in her or his face as the "great doubt block." Everything that the student believes he or she has left behind suddenly appears directly in front as a massive and immovable boulder, blocking any further progress. It is as though, in attempting to transcend his or her ego, the student has in fact been consolidating his or her distinctiveness. The work of inquiring into the koan has been appropriated by the ego as evidence of the student's commitment and spiritual worthiness to gain satori. Any attempt to move the boulder only adds to its size, and sets it more firmly in place.

In order to force the student into an experience of the great doubt, koan practice is combined with the practice of zazen. This combination produces a potent and highly charged environment in which the chances of achieving breakthrough insight are greatly enhanced. On top of the regular daily practice are frequent periods of still more intensified koan work called *sesshin*. During these periods, the student meditates for up to eighteen hours a day and is required to have a formal interview (*sanzen*) with the master a number of times each day, in which he or she offers a solution to the koan. At times, the intensity and seeming significance of these encounters are such that the student has to be forcibly dragged into the master's room by other students. As Richard De Martino remarks:

Under the stimulation of such a regimen with its taut and serious atmosphere, the given koan may begin to take effect. The student, prodded by the stick of the head monk when dozing comes upon him, exertion wanes, or stiffness and tiredness set in, and spurred, inspired, goaded or even driven by the master, finds himself to be more and more caught by his koan. As his each response to it is rejected, he becomes increasing dislodged, shaken, and unsteady in whatever assurance or complacency he originally had.[36]

The koan takes on the dimensions of a life-and-death struggle for the ego. "The koan thus comes to be . . . a living crisis, taking over as the central and exclusive concern of . . . [the student's] entire being."[37]

In working with a koan, the Zen student attempts to keep his or her inquiry active at all times. The student becomes totally obsessed by the koan. Every attempt to solve the puzzle intellectually is rejected by the master. But the search goes on unabated and with ever-increasing intensity. The bankruptcy of the mind in the search for a solution places the student under tremendous pressure. The ego "holding onto this last remnant of itself . . . feels that it can still, at least for the present, preserve itself, albeit in an almost intolerable condition."[38] "The ego, in an existential quandary which it can neither compose, endure, abandon, or escape, is unable to advance, unable to retreat, unable to stand fixed."[39] Yet the master continues unrelentingly to demand that the student resolve this insane predicament. The master demands that the student fully experience and live the contradiction that being an ego entails.

Finally, when the student is at the point of total and utter desperation, the intellect can break open and allow the nature of the mind itself to appear in a satori experience. This represents a cataclysmic breakdown of the ego's defenses, in which the student simultaneously dies and is reborn as simply a focus of awareness. The student is irrevocably propelled into an infinitely more spacious and unrestricted level of awareness in a "great awakening." Mind gives way to no-mind, and from here on the student allows the experience to permeate his or her entire being.

4

Tantra—
Dynamic Transformation

Before we move on to look at non-orthodox approaches to spiritual development, we must at least briefly survey the rich Tantric tradition, for there is now no doubt that Tantra will make a major contribution to the shape of Western Buddhism in coming centuries.

There is perhaps a tendency to identify Tantra exclusively with Tibetan Buddhism, but, in fact, Tantric traditions are also known in Chinese, Japanese, and Korean Buddhism. However, the most accessible and best known of the Tantric traditions is without doubt the Tibetan, and my remarks here therefore apply to Tibetan Tantra.

Although the Chinese annexation and invasion of Tibet in the 1950s is an ongoing tragedy of catastrophic proportions for all Tibetans, the resulting diaspora relocated hundreds of Tibet's highest lamas to India and the West, whence the remoteness of Tibet is no longer an obstacle to spiritual seekers attracted to Tibetan Buddhism. Within a blink of forty years, Tantric traditions that had been guarded and concealed for over a thousand years have become readily accessible in every major metropolis in the Americas, Europe, and Australasia—surely this phenomenon will stand as one of the most remarkable events in Buddhism's 2,500 year history. Many leading lamas, including His Holiness the Dalai Lama, have said that Tantra is suited to the West and that the West is ready for

Tantra. The highly influential Kagyudpa lama, Chögyam Trungpa, went so far as to say that the United States is Tantra!

The Tantric tradition emerged initially as a secret—and in a sense, perhaps, spiritually subversive—movement, drawing adherents from both Hindu and Buddhist yogic communities. It challenged the orthodoxy of the monastic institutions by creating a countercultural alternative, based on informal communities of forest ascetics and lay yogins and yoginis. The Tantras themselves were taught by distinct lineages or powerful adepts, who were part of a predominantly oral tradition.

By its very nature, early Tantra has left little material on which to base any sort of history—it is not even certain when the movement arose, although it was in existence by the fourth century C. E., and may well date to earlier times.[1] As Tantra became more spiritually mainstream, it developed distinctly Hindu and Buddhist styles, primarily through the work of philosophers who were concerned to establish it on sound conceptual foundations that were consistent with their own philosophical frameworks.

In some ways, Buddhist Tantra or Vajrayana grew out of a certain impatience with the social propriety and institutional conservatism of the Mahayana tradition. Certainly, in India, Mahayana Buddhism quite quickly became the property of philosopher-monks, each arguing for the superiority of his own interpretations of the state of buddhahood. For other followers of the *Dharma*, however, the raw and unpredictable energy of human emotions and relationships suggested a different and more dynamic path to enlightenment, one that fully embraced the passions, delusions, and neuroses of human existence, rather than ignoring or suppressing them. As Chögyam Trungpa Rinpoche puts it: "If you are highly involved in one emotion such as anger . . . you begin to see that you do not have to suppress your energy. You do not have to keep calm and suppress the energy of anger, but you can transform your aggression into dynamic energy."[2]

Although Tantra is routinely presented as an unorthodox form of Buddhism, here we must categorize it as an orthodox system, since, as we shall see, it involves the application of a method with the expectation that a result will be achieved in the course of time (albeit, in some cases, a brief time).

TANTRIC LITERATURE

Like all Buddhist traditions, Tantra has a large and heterogeneous corpus of literature, the content of which ranges from metaphysical or philosophical material to instruction on meditation practice, details of the performance of rites and ceremonies, and particulars of certain types of magic operation. It also includes a large body of commentarial work. Among the principal Tantras, we may note the *Guhyasamaja Tantra*, generally regarded as one of the oldest of the Tantras; the *Chakrasamvara Tantra*; the *Hevajra Tantra*; the *Mañjushrimalakalpa*; and the *Kalachakra Tantra*, perhaps the most complex and intricate of the Tantras. Much of this material has been lost in the original languages and survives only in Tibetan translation.

Scholars vary widely in their estimates of the age of given Tantric texts, but it is improbable that any of them were committed to writing before the fourth century C. E., and most of them date from a much later period. Very little Tantric literature has been translated into Western languages, a fact in part attributable to the nature of the language in which they are written, for Tantric writing makes wide use of abstruse symbolism, ambiguity, cryptic allusion, and highly specialized vocabulary. Many Tantric texts are thus impossible to understand without the guidance of a master skilled in the practice of the teachings. Only in recent times has a generation of Western scholars arisen whose personal experience of Tantric practice equips them to undertake the work of providing Western-language versions of these texts.

A FRUITION PATH

While the spiritual goals of Tantra and Mahayana are the same—namely, the fully evolved state of buddhahood—the two traditions approach that goal from different points of view. Tantra is traditionally defined as a "fruition path," in contrast to the Mahayana and Theravada, which are known as "causal paths." In the causal paths, the practitioner tries to create the causes for later enlightenment by engaging in virtuous and productive activities, such as the four jhanas, and the various stages of the Mahayana path. The assumption is that these actions will produce a result at some time in the future, in the same way as planting a seed will eventually produce a fully grown plant. "Some time in the future," however, may be a very long time indeed, for it may take eons to achieve full enlightenment.

In the fruition path, on the other hand, the state of buddhahood is imagined as a present reality. Rather than working patiently for a future result, in Tantra we create the result right here and now; we simulate the state of full awakening in this and every moment. The simulation of this state is achieved through highly dynamic meditations in which the Tantric practitioner or *tantrika* seeks to reconstitute the mind-body so that it is the mind-body of a buddha, engaging in enlightened activities and living in an enlightened world. Every dimension of existence is enhanced, expanded, and elevated to the point where there is no difference between the simulated experience and the reality of being a buddha living in a pure spiritual universe inhabited by other spiritually evolved beings.

Solid practitioners will engage each day in a range of Tantric meditations that might take two or three hours to complete. Advanced practitioners consolidate their Tantric practice through retreats—in Tibetan Tantra, there is a tradition of completing solitary retreats lasting three (in fact, closer to three and a half) years. There are many Tibetan yogis and lamas who have completed one or more of these three-year retreats. In recent times, a number of Westerners have also completed the three-year retreat.

The Tantric path is both very fast and very dangerous because of the level of energy involved. It requires great skill to successfully negotiate this path, because there is a very fine line to tread in acting as if one is enlightened, without deluding oneself that one actually is. The main safeguard against these dangers is one's reliance on a fully qualified teacher (*guru*) in a system that is largely secret, and closed to the uninitiated.[3]

The practice of Tantra uses three main tools: visualization; the use of physical gestures and postures (*mudra*); and the utterance of sacred sounds (*mantra*). These tools represent different channels of sensory stimulation that are creatively modified in meditative practice in order to simulate the experience and environment of an enlightened being.

In the Tantric tradition the mind is viewed as inherently endowed with the awakened qualities of buddhahood. Buddhahood is our authentic state. Our normal experience of being confused, limited, and dissatisfied isn't real. We fail to see "things as they really are." Our ordinary perception delivers us a distorted and impoverished experience of a multidimensional universe that is pure, luminous, open, and dynamic, and in which we have the light-filled appearance of an enlightened being. According to Tantra, then, our authentic state has been obscured by the distortions of our mental defilements.

Whereas in Mahayana practice cognitive structures are deconstructed in order to reveal an experience of pure, unstructured awareness, in Tantra, mental defilements themselves are transmuted into the fundamental energy of embodied awareness. Ignorance, for example, is transformed in the omnipresent wisdom of the ultimate sphere, anger into mirror-like wisdom, pride into the wisdom of equanimity, desire into discriminating wisdom, and jealousy into all-accomplishing wisdom. When this transformation is complete, the mind is realized as suchness.[4] Thus, in the words of Sahajayoginichinta, an eighth-century female Tantric poet and practitioner:

> *Activities that are graceful, heroic, terrifying,*
> *Compassionate, furious, and peaceful—*
> *And passion, anger, greed, pride, and envy—*
> *All these things without exception*
> *Are the perfect forms*
> *Of pure, self-illuminating wisdom.*[5]

The Tantric path is therefore based upon the transformation of these defilements into their authentic state, in particular through discovering that the three fundamental aspects of buddhahood (*trikaya*) are inherent within our minds. These three aspects are *dharmakaya*, buddhahood in its pure, absolute state; *sambhogakaya*, buddhahood as perceived by bodhisattvas and other spiritually evolved beings; and *nirmanakaya*, buddhahood as perceived by unenlightened beings. Since buddhahood is our authentic state, these three modes of buddhahood refer also to three modes of reality: the *dharmakaya* is the very essence and nature of reality, while the sambhogakaya is a transcendent perception of reality, and nirmanakaya is a numinous perception. In Tantric practice, all beings are seen as manifestations of the nirmanakaya, endowed with the qualities and virtues of bodhisattvas; all sounds resonate with the symbolism of the sambhogakaya; and all thoughts are a display of the ultimately real, the dharmakaya.[6]

Thus, instead of focusing on the shortcomings and miseries of samsara, in Tantra the world is viewed as a pure manifestation of awakened activity. Tantric practitioners view themselves as deities possessing all the awakened qualities of a buddha. The physical world is experienced as a divine mansion (mandala), and within that mansion all things sparkle with intimations of ultimate reality, all things are endowed with the deepest of significance. All sound— be it speech, bird song, the clamor of construction work or the roar of city traffic—is transformed into the vibrations of sacred sounds (mantra). All activity in the universe expresses the dynamics of enlightenment (mudra), and all visual sensations are manifestations of the primordial teacher (*guru*).

In Tantric literature, this elevated viewpoint is referred to as "pure perception." Thus, when desire arises in the yogin's mind, it is experienced as the arising of a deity, and the practitioner relates to this emotion as the deity. In this way, desire comes to be experienced without any taint of egocentric associations. Through repeated training, the Tantric practitioner uproots his or her habitual tendency to perpetuate dualistic mind, and begins to function as an awakened being.[7] Gradually, all oppositions come to be subsumed in a state of indivisible unity. The single overriding commitment in

Tantra is to hold this pure perception, consistently and continuously, twenty-four hours a day, without lapsing into ordinary, contaminated perception for even a second.

NONDUALITY IN TANTRA

According to the Tantra, the dualistic categories of subject and object, sacred and profane, samsara and nirvana are all mind-produced. In reality, there is only the ultimate sphere of reality. Because the sphere of reality is utterly pure, uncompounded, and all pervasive, it is said to be "nondual."[8] In Tantra, the idea of nonduality is mainly explained in terms of "union" and "spontaneous coemergence."[9] "Union" means that the two levels of reality, ultimate and relative—in other words, nirvana and samsara—are not two separate things. "Spontaneous coemergence" acknowledges that nirvana and samsara are dependent on each other. Tantric texts don't speak about nirvana in a way that would encourage people to seek out a dualistic form of liberation by rejecting the complexities of samsara. Rather, they point to the reality within which samsara and nirvana—the experiences of unalloyed bliss and extricating suffering—are equalized and transcended by connecting with the ground of all being. Because this state precedes both confusion and wisdom, samsara and nirvana have no meaning in relation to it.

CREATION AND COMPLETION PRACTICES

The Tantric path is divided into two phases. The first of these is called the "Creation Phase," because it is based on constructive forms of meditation. The second is the "Fulfillment Phase," which utilizes nondual yogic awareness.

The central practice in the Creation Phase is deity yoga. This involves visualizing oneself as an enlightened being inhabiting a spiritual universe (*mandala*). The meditative literature provides detailed descriptions of spiritual universes, which are used as models for constructing one's own sacred space. In these practices, tantrikas revision the entire perceptual world by vividly imaging that they reside as the central enlightened figure in a divine palace made of vibrating light energy and inhabited by other enlightened beings. As Kennard Lipman writes, "Through visualizing and embodying this dimension, experiencing oneself as a luminous presence in a palace of light, one transforms one's ordinary situation of the body as the focus of drives and obsessions. . . ."[10]

Numerous deities exist in the Tantric systems, each one of which has particular attributes, characteristics, and appearance. Each deity represents an aspect of the practitioner's own psyche. A different relationship is cultivated with the deity depending on one's level of practice.[11] At the beginning of these practices, one imagines that the deity is outside of oneself, while in the later stages one imagines that there is no separation between oneself and the deity. One develops "divine pride" through knowing that one is endowed with the appearance, speech, and actions of a fully evolved being. The aim of this practice is to attain the form of the deity as the unity of appearance and openness. In this way, the duality between enlightened and unenlightened, sacred and ordinary, is gradually eroded.

In a typical practice session, meditators visualize themselves as having the form and attire of a particular enlightened being, and they reinforce that perception by using the mantras and mudras associated with that being. This new self-image is idealized in the sense that it is often adorned with certain symbols representing different aspects of the enlightened being's personality (style of dress, for example, personal ornaments and accoutrements, posture, and so on); and the simulated beings themselves symbolize qualities such as compassion, wisdom, and spiritual power. As practitioners become adept at this form of meditation, their practice takes on a life of its own. The visualized reality progressively displaces the ordinary view that they have of themselves. Similarly, the mantras begin to resonate of their own accord without the need for meditators to intone them consciously. The characteristics of the enlightened being with which practitioners seek to identify re-integrate their personality structure, moving it in the direction of a being

who embodies perfect wisdom, complete compassion, and indestructible power.

At the beginning, practitioners sense only the faintest outlines of
this new and spectacular environment, but after years of solitary
meditation, they can instantly bring into being a panorama of
translucent imagery, pulsating with the energy and activity of a
realm inhabited only by enlightened beings. Although this process
begins as a meditative exercise, the effects gradually alter practitioners' experience of the everyday world, so that it takes on a less hos-
tile and polluted aspect. They come to see themselves and others "in
their best light," and respond accordingly. What was originally a fabrication, a simulation, becomes real as meditators activate a feedback loop that reinforces their new reality.

THE HIGHEST YOGA TANTRAS

At the highest level of Tantra, *Annutarayogatantra*, practitioners
dig into the most intense and darkest aspects of their anxieties,
fantasies, and desires. They use their fear, anger, and sexual drive in
order to channel the most powerful emotional energies available to
them in the service of developing and communicating their
enlightened awareness. For example, in order to transmute and liberate the shadow dimensions of their personalities, they visualize
fierce and terrifyingly configured deities. The aim in identifying
with these forms is to carefully release the tremendous amount of
energy that is trapped within these negative and socially destruc-
tive emotions, and transmute this energy into the life-force of a
cosmic deity by infusing it with the liberating wisdom of openness.
Also, at this level the deities are always visualized in sexual union,
symbolizing the indivisible unity of subject and object, bliss and
openness, compassion and wisdom. The emphasis on cultivating
experiences of bliss may sound like anathema to Buddhism, but as
Thubten Yeshe explains: "[T]antric practitioners use the energy of
their own pleasure as a resource and, in the deep concentration of
samadhi meditation, unify it with the wisdom that realizes

emptiness. . . . The person who is qualified to practice Tantra is able to cope with pleasure, to experience pleasure without losing control, to utilize it. This is the essential characteristic of the Tantric personality."[12]

The second phase on the Tantric Path is called the "Fulfillment Phase," and all Highest Yoga Tantras are associated with the Fulfillment Phase practices. In this final level, meditators dissolve the constructed experience of a deity back into the experience of undifferentiated awareness, and rest in a state of non-conceptualization.[13] In part, the intention is to correct any tendency to think that Buddhist deities are anything more than created realities. However, here the fulfillment practice involves diverting and controlling psycho-physical energies within the nervous system in order to provide a more direct neurological support for the visionary and nondual experiences of Tantra. This is called working with the "indestructible body" (*vajrakaya*).[14] This includes esoteric practices such as dream yoga, the generation of internal heat through a practice called *chandali*, and yogas that use dying and death as processes for rapid spiritual advancement.[15] Ayurveda, Chinese Taoism, and Indo-Tibetan Tantra maintain that there is a subtle and intricate system of energy pathways within and around the body, giving us vitality and accounting for illness, psychological imbalance, and spiritual vitality and stagnation. According to these systems, our thoughts and emotions are tied to the flow of energy within this subtle system. If the energies are constricted, blocked, or unbalanced, they produce physical illness, confusion, and emotional conflicts. Practitioners generate meditative experiences of sublime bliss and openness by controlling the movement of energy within the channels, through physical postures, breath control, and visualization practices.

• • •

We have given here only the simplest of sketches of the Buddhist Tantric tradition. The practices are extremely varied, and can become highly complex as one moves through many levels of practice designed to transform the contaminated and contaminating environment into a pure and blissful universe.

Within the practice of deity yoga, Tantric practitioners continue to develop their wisdom and compassion. Their meditations are all framed and motivated by *bodhichitta*—the aspiration and intention to bring all creatures to full awakening. And in the context of their Tantric *sadhana*, practitioners continue to meditate on openness by deconstructing any tendency to view "the deity" as real and independent.

5

Dzogchen and Mahamudra— Beyond Practice

Having outlined the approaches of the orthodox Buddhist traditions, we come now to the unorthodox. In illustrating the unorthodox approach, it would be equally legitimate to focus on Dzogchen, Mahamudra or certain aspects of early Ch'an/Zen. In fact, masters of the Kadam and Sakya schools of Tibetan Buddhism recognized the similarity of these traditions as early as the 12th century. Several masters of these schools accuse Dzogchen and Mahamudra practitioners of leading their students astray.[1] The great Sakyapa scholar Sakya Pandita, in particular, accused both Dzogchen and Mahamudra of being illegitimate systems because they were not based upon Indian Tantric traditions. He also criticized them on account of their doctrinal similarities to Ch'an.[2]

In this chapter, we will say a little about Mahamudra and in the next we will highlight the unorthodox features of Zen. For the most part, however, we will focus on the Dzogchen tradition. The main reason for this emphasis is that Dzogchen has become the prime avenue through which Western practitioners are accessing and identifying the unorthodox perspective. In the West, Dzogchen is very much the "flavor of the decade," and any reference to the tradition is a good selling-point for many seekers, for Dzogchen also seems to have the capacity to present itself as a more pure and distinctive expression of the discourse of immediacy than does Mahamudra or Zen.

It is useful to note in passing the meanings of the terms *Dzogchen* and *Mahamudra*. *Dzogchen* is often translated as "Great" (*chen*) "Perfection" (*dzog*), but it can just as accurately be translated as "Complete" or "Total Fulfillment." In both cases, the term points to an experience of reality that simply cannot be enhanced any further, because it transcends all notions of perfection or imperfection. The term *Mahamudra* can be explained in various ways, but it is usually translated as "Great" (*maha*) "Seal" (*mudra*), because it "seals" every conceivable experience—the objective and the subjective, the spiritual and the ordinary—with the liberating wisdom of openness. This seal of Mahamudra bridges and transcends dualistic categories. It is unimpeded, because it encompasses both samsara and nirvana. It cannot be limited by any experience or idea.

•   •   •

At the outset, we should acknowledge that Dzogchen and Mahamudra don't really exist at the present time as unique traditions. Although both are products of the Indian spiritual landscape, they are now accessed exclusively through the Nyingma and Kagyud traditions of Tibetan Buddhism, respectively. Within these traditions, they are tightly integrated with the orthodox systems of Tibetan Tantra. Consequently, it is now impossible to extract pure expressions of these traditions. This was not always the case, however. In India, for example, at the time of the great *siddha* Saraha,[3] there existed a distinct Mahamudra tradition that explicitly dispensed with the transformational practices of Tantra, advocating instead the direct apprehension of the mind by dropping all contrived spiritual activity.[4] In a song to Maitripa, the Tibetan translator Marpa refers to this as "Naked Mahamudra."[5] It is also referred to as the "Middle Way of Non-fabrication." According to Gampopa, this strictly nondual form of Mahamudra was superior to both sutra and tantra.[6] Similarly, Dzogchen is not normally approached in the Tibetan traditions until the practitioner has gained extensive experience in Tantric practice.

A HIDDEN TRADITION

Paradoxically, Dzogchen is simultaneously one of the most profound yet least distinctive traditions of Buddhism. Its obscurity may in part be explained by its deeply experiential nature, together with the fact that it was traditionally a highly esoteric and sophisticated teaching. The Tibetans who practiced this tradition only communicated it to a small number of students who they considered were able to implement and embody the teaching without distorting it.

Strictly speaking, Dzogchen cannot be identified by pointing to any single text, any unique philosophical position, any special ritual, or any particular institution. While the Tibetan Dzogchen tradition has produced a comprehensive body of literature and meditative practice, these are regarded as paraphernalia, since in its essence, Dzogchen amounts simply to understanding the fundamental nature of mind, which transcends thought and language, yet doesn't exclude their operation.

Dzogchen characterizes itself as a spiritual perspective that has been tapped into from beginningless time by hidden yogis and yoginis who have seen through the cognitive and emotional structures that separate reality into experiences of the sublime and mundane, pleasure and pain, the veridical and illusory, without subsequently constructing their insight as any sort of spiritual achievement. In the Dzogchen tradition, this is referred to as "the uncontrived realization of things-as-they-are." This experience goes beyond the need for any practice, and stands outside of any institutions, since there is nothing that needs to be maintained, nor anything that needs to be destroyed. Thus, symbolically, Dzogchen's origins are said to lie in the primordial and eternal buddha-mind, *Samantabhadra*, which rare individuals realize as none other than their own essential nature.

Dzogchen emerged during the seventh to tenth centuries within the Tantric mysticism traditions of North West India and Tibet.[7] The first master to be associated with the tradition was Vajraprahe, more commonly known under his Tibetan name, Garab Dorje.[8] The tradition was then transmitted through various Indian masters such as Mañjushrimitra, Vairochana, Padmasambhava, Vimalamitra, Shrisimha, and Jnanasutra.[9]

The Dzogchen tradition reached Tibet during the seventh century in the "First Transmission"[10] of Buddhist teachings, and was integrated into the practices of the Nyingma or "Old School" of Tibetan Buddhism. The Mahamudra tradition emerged at the same time through a different lineage of Indian masters, including Saraha (eighth or early ninth century), Savaripa (eighth century), Tilopa (988–1069) and Maitripa (1010–1087). It was brought to Tibet by Marpa and there transmitted to Naropa (1016–1100), Milarepa (1040–1123), and Gampopa (1079–1153), who are regarded as among the founders of the Kagyud school.

As noted, both traditions—Dzogchen and Mahamudra—were integrated with the complex transformational practices of Tantra. The Nyingma school regards Dzogchen as the capstone of the complex and detailed system of training that begins with the Hinayana, progresses to the Mahayana and finally works its way through the various levels of Tantra;[11] Mahamudra occupies a similar position in the Kagyud school.

Even so, these traditions tend to stand outside of the orthodox religious institutions. Indian and Tibetan hagiographical literature are rich with uplifting stories about Dzogchen and Mahamudra practitioners who began their spiritual life as celibate monks, then moved out of their cloistered institutions into the wider community, where they became independent—and in some cases highly controversial—exponents of the path of natural freedom.

Many of the great practitioners of Dzogchen were anonymous hermits and recluses who lived in mountain caves, while others were nomads, living with their extended families and tending herds of yaks on the steppes of the Tibetan plateau. Others were politicians, administrators, traders, or even beggars; yet others occupied high positions in Tibet's religious hierarchy, in both the Nyingma and other traditions. The Fifth Dalai Lama, for example, was a Dzogchen practitioner, although he, like all the Dalai Lamas, belonged to the more scholastically inclined Gelug tradition, which has at times tended to disparage the Dzogchen tradition.

More than any other of Tibet's Buddhist traditions, Dzogchen cuts across social, religious, and economic divisions. And it has crossed gender divisions: while certain Buddhist traditions have from time to time shown misogynist tendencies, Dzogchen has always appealed strongly to women, and, indeed, has probably produced more female teachers than the other Buddhist traditions. The non-institutional and communal nature of Dzogchen has much to do with this. As Tsultrim Allione notes, "Dzog chen communities tend to be non-hierarchical, based on cooperation rather than competition, communities of families or loosely formed collections of hermits of both sexes who have no particular 'organizations' but who help and support each other without any imposing hierarchies."[12]

The Dzogchen and Mahamudra traditions are unique on many counts. In their purest expressions, they reject any attempt to stimulate spiritual awakening through study, ritual, prayer, or any other praxis, including meditation. In fact, they systematically deconstruct the discourses that validate these spiritual methods. They also claim that the types of spiritual experiences that can be produced by such methods are spiritually valueless, or even of negative worth. They are valueless because the ultimate state has no structure and hence cannot be a specific experience as such.

The source of these traditions rests in a timeless, transpersonal experience of unstructured awareness so they are also transcultural and transhistorical. This means that there is no necessary connection between Dzogchen and Buddhism. Dzogchen has existed, and continues to exist, independently of Buddhism, in the same way that some Zen practitioners feel no connection to Buddhism. According to Dzogchen, the relationship between Dzogchen and Buddhism is contingent,[13] and Dzogchen was, and still is, cultivated within the indigenous Bön tradition.[14] Dzogchen's historical affiliation with Buddhism can be attributed to the fact that Buddhism supplies a very fertile and conducive foundation for the exploration of spiritual experience that transcends the need for beliefs, rituals, and even scriptures. Buddhism provides a supporting link because of its own emphasis on the primacy of direct experience.

NOTHING TO DO

The eleventh-century female master, Niguma, provides a concise description of Mahamudra that is equally applicable to Dzogchen:

> *Don't do anything whatsoever with the mind—*
> *Abide in an authentic, natural state.*
> *One's own mind, unwavering, is the Dharmakaya.*
> *The key is to meditate like this without wavering;*
> *Experience the great [reality] beyond extremes.*
>
> *In a pellucid ocean,*
> *Bubbles arise and dissolve again.*
> *Just so, thoughts are no different from ultimate reality,*
> *So don't find fault; remain at ease.*
> *Whatever arises, whatever occurs,*
> *Don't grasp—release it on the spot.*
> *Appearances, sounds and objects are one's own mind;*
> *There's nothing except mind.*
> *Mind is beyond the extremes of birth and death.*
> *The nature of mind, awareness,*
> *Although using the objects of the five senses,*
> *Does not wander from reality.*
>
> *In the state of cosmic equilibrium*
> *There is nothing to abandon or practice,*
> *No meditation or post-meditation period.*[15]

According to the unorthodox traditions, then, there is nothing to accomplish and nowhere to go, for there are no gaps between what we already are and what we aspire to be. The buddha-mind is no different from the mind of a deluded sentient being. Consequently there is no real separation between the nature of deluded thoughts and the quality of awakened presence.[16] The three aspects of buddhahood are our "natural state," whereby everything that we could wish to accomplish is already immanent within us. Thus in another of the Mahamudra texts, we read:

The intrinsic nature of the ordinary mind is supreme fruition.
If maintained without modulating
It is the threefold enlightenment [trikaya];
If let go of, it is ultimate awareness . . .
It is the mother of the buddhas throughout the three periods
    of time.[17]

It is interesting to find precursors of this view in the earliest known Buddhist teachings. Thus in the Pali Canon, the Buddha says, "Luminous, O monks, is the mind; and it is defiled by adventitious defilements. Luminous, O monks, is the mind, and it is free from adventitious defilements."[18] Here, the first statement refers to the condition of the unenlightened mind, while the second refers to the mind's natural state of luminosity.

The idea that these defilements are "adventitious" obscurations over an inherently pure mind is further developed in certain Mahayana texts—thus both the *Srimaladevi* and *Ratnagotravibhaga* (*Mahayanuttaratantra Shastra*) describe the defilements as having the same nature as the mind. In fact, the defilements are unable to stain the mind in any way because the mind is already complete and perfect within itself, whence there is no need to follow a path or to eradicate mental impurities. As the *Ratnagotravibhaga* states: "There is nothing whatsoever to be removed from this, nor the slightest thing thereon to add. Truly beholding the true nature— when truly seen—complete liberation."[19] Similar ideas are found in the Prajnaparamita literature.

However, it is in the unorthodox traditions that the implications of this teaching are applied to their fullest. According to these traditions, we do not need to do anything to manufacture awakening because our natural state has been completely pure right from the beginning. As the Dzogchen master Longchenpa says, "In the rootless Mind, pure from the beginning, there is nothing to do and no one to do it—how satisfying![20]

The Dzogchen tradition therefore differs from the orthodox approaches we have outlined in that it doesn't provide a path. One doesn't traverse any territory on this approach, but this does not mean that one has arrived at the culmination of spiritual journey. Thus, one of the primary Dzogchen texts, the *All Creating King*, describes Dzogchen in terms of the Ten Absences:

1. There is no view on which one has to meditate.

2. There is no commitment, or samaya, one has to keep.

3. There is no capacity for spiritual action one has to seek.

4. There is no mandala one has to create.

5. There is no initiation one has to receive.

6. There is no path one has to tread.

7. There are no levels of realization (*bhumis*) one has to achieve through purification.

8. There is no conduct one has to adopt, or abandon.

9. From the beginning, self-arising wisdom has been free of obstacle.

10. Self-perfection is beyond hope or fear.[21]

Here there is nothing to gain or lose, because the experience transcends the need to avoid suffering, or achieve liberation. Nothing contradicts or threatens this experience, since everything that one has ever thought, done, or experienced is an expression of a state of complete fulfillment.

Similarly, according to Mahamudra, there is nothing to achieve because the state of realization is inherent within the "ordinary mind." Gampopa describes ordinary mind as a self-cognizing awareness that has never been stained by empirical consciousness or conceptual thought, and which is free of all philosophical views.[22] This ordinary mind is "nonabiding," because it is not an entity. It cannot be located and cannot be said to exist or not exist. As Maitripa sings in his *Songs on View, Meditation, Action and Fruit*:

> *Outer and Inner are simultaneously arising.*
> *This non-conceptual yoga is like the flow of a river.*

As one need search nowhere other than mind,
The path of mahamudra is non-activity of mind.
If you have no thought of hope for the fruit, it is mahamudra.
If you have no thought of non-thought, thoughts are like clouds
*   in the sky.*
If you understand this, their nature is empty.
View, meditation, action, and fruit are inseparable and
*   simultaneously arising,*
If you realise non-duality, this is the supreme fruit—
*   buddhahood.*[23]

NATURAL LIBERATION

In the Dzogchen tradition, reactive emotions and burdensome thoughts are said to release or liberate themselves. In contrast to the orthodox paths, "one does not contrive or condition [one's mind] by suppressing [one's experiences], or [applying] remedies, but lets [the mind] rest naturally in whatever [condition one finds it]."[24] The contemporary Dzogchen master, Namkhai Norbu Rinpoche, explains further:

> When we speak of the path of self-liberation, there is neither a concept of renunciation, because if it is always my energy manifesting, then it can manifest in many different ways: nor is there a concept of transformation, because the principle here is that I find myself in a state of pure presence, of contemplation. If I find myself for an instant in a state of contemplation, then from that point of view, wrath and compassion are one and the same. Good and evil are one and same. In that condition there is nothing to do; one liberates oneself, because one finds oneself in one's own dimension of energy without escaping and without renouncing anything. This is the principle of self-liberation.[25]

Self-liberation, or the spontaneous release of reactive emotions, occurs as a natural consequence of identifying with awareness-as-such. When one's awareness ceases to be conditioned by compulsively or intentionally engaging and disengaging with different sensations, then thoughts and feelings float through one's awareness like clouds in the sky. Emotions dissolve like snow falling on the warm water of one's panoramic awareness.

The ability to spontaneously liberate constricting emotions and compulsive thoughts rests on neither grasping at nor suppressing any arising thought, feeling, or perception. As Longchenpa, writes, "One doesn't discard [some experiences] and cultivate [others]. [Whether one's experiences] are dynamic or stable one should let them go wherever they want to go….When the mind is in a diffusing or dynamic state one isn't discouraged, and when it is calm and stable one desists from wanting [it to continue in that state]."26

Consequently, one doesn't judge some experiences as sublime and others as profane. One doesn't make more out of one's experience than what is immediately given. One doesn't enhance or accentuate one's experience, as one does in Tantra; but neither does one trivialize or devalue it. Basically, one doesn't intervene in or meddle with one's experience in any way at all. One's experience is natural, unaffected, unmanipulated, and free from contrivance. This practice is called "leaving what appears just as it is."

PURE, UNSTRUCTURED AWARENESS

In the unorthodox traditions, the only practice—which cannot be practiced anyway—is simply being present and aware in the moment.27 This bare experience of the present moment is often described as "nonmeditation," because it is natural and uncontrived. As the Indian siddha Savaripa writes in his *Collection of Songs on the Oral Mahamudra Teachings*:

Kye Ho!
Non-meditation is non-activity of mind.
The natural state of ordinary mind
Is spoilt by contrived concentration.
In naturally pure mind, effort is unnecessary.

When you neither hold it nor let it wander it rests by itself.
If you do not understand, meditation is pointless.
By understanding this you transcend meditator and
    meditation-object.
When a thought arises just see its nature.
Do not conceive the water and waves to be different.
In the Mahamudra of non-activity of mind
There is not even an atom upon which to meditate.
Not being separate from non-meditation is the supreme
    meditation.[28]

In these traditions, there is no meditative concentration or deliberate attentiveness, because any form of mental focus or conscious intentionality only serves to distort and displace the uncontrived nature of unstructured awareness. In Mahamudra, for example, "the word 'meditation' is merely given to the act of acquainting mind with the meaning of the natural state. . . . You never meditate by fabricating something mentally, such as a concrete object with color or shape. Nor should you deliberately meditate while suppressing the mind's thinking or perceptions, as in meditation on a constructed emptiness. Meditation means simply sustaining the naturalness of your mind without any fabrication."[29]

Nor is there a need either to refute or to establish any views, truths, or theses, because experience isn't influenced by one's beliefs. In this way, one becomes free from the duality of cognition and cognizer, and thus remains in a free state of non-appraisal. Neither is it necessary to remove thoughts or emotions in order to achieve freedom. What is required is that one no longer be conditioned by thoughts and emotions. As Namkhai Norbu Rinpoche writes:

One's passions only grow powerful because one is ignorant of the state of pure presence, and so consequently one follows after one's passions. But when one finds oneself in the state of the pure presence of the passions, one is not dominated by them nor does one have to suppress them because they are like the ornaments of one's primordial state. Thus one's passions are self-liberated into their own condition whenever they arise.[30]

When bare awareness has been activated, thoughts and emotions no longer function as conditioning agents. Even though one may engage in thinking and be subject to emotional responses, thoughts and emotions no longer cause or condition one's present and future mental states. Thoughts and feelings arise, but are freed in the sense that they are merely a presence or happening, occurring within the real dimension of one's being.

The only discipline in Dzogchen is to stay in a natural and unfabricated state of bare awareness. A very important and in some respects quite complex issue in Tantra is commitment, or *samaya*, which involves among other things the maintenance of the connection with one's teacher and lineage, and the firm resolution to persevere with whichever practice one is involved in. In Dzogchen, however, the single commitment is to be aware, knowing both that one cannot do this, and that awareness itself is not an existing thing. As Namkhai Norbu Rinpoche writes:

> There are many kinds of [commitment]: in the mahayoga, for example, there are fourteen main ones. . . . However, in Dzogchen the principle is different. When, in daily life, one remains in the natural state, abiding in awareness and presence, there are no rules to observe, there is nothing specific one has to do: it is enough not to get distracted, remaining in present awareness. . . . In Dzogchen, commitment is not something one has to uphold with effort because the nature of the state of consciousness is the unborn, beyond all limitations. . . .[31]

Nevertheless, the earlier paths do come into play in Dzogchen, because the cultivation and maintenance of this awareness is achieved by avoiding the opposing states of drowsiness and elation. Behaviorally, this means that practitioners of Dzogchen avoid actions and environments that stimulate depression, boredom, lethargy, excitement, agitation, and so on. However, once one is in that state, there is nothing that one can do either to enhance it or destroy it. Furthermore, one sees that all the effort one has applied to gain this experience has neither contributed to, nor detracted from, its occurrence, since it is the primordial and unconditioned nature of being as such.

•   •   •

Dzogchen goes further than presenting a perspective that transcends the need for spiritual practice, for in Dzogchen, we encounter a radical and thoroughgoing critique of the orthodox framework discussed in the first chapters of this book. Because this critique strikes at the very heart of all forms of goal-oriented practice, it is appropriate to call this the "anti-method critique." This forms the topic of the next chapter.

6

Anti-Method

In earlier chapters, we considered a number of different types of
practice used within orthodox forms of Buddhism to facilitate the
development of spiritual insight, and in the previous chapter, we
briefly discussed the underpinnings of the unorthodox perspective
offered by Dzogchen and other traditions. Within its own frame of
reference, each tradition makes complete sense, and real, tangible
benefits seem to accrue to practitioners with each of these systems.

Anyone who has spent time in Theravada monasteries in
Southeast Asia, or joined programs and retreats at Western Insight
Meditation centers, can attest to the atmosphere of composure and
serenity that pervades these communities. There also seems little
doubt that notching up one or two decades of mindfulness practice
greatly enhances our ability to accommodate uncertainty and
change, and increases our capacity to handle difficult feelings and
emotions.

Mahayana practice is similarly able to relieve human suffering
and reorient people's lives, giving them a larger and more meaningful vision of human existence. Perhaps the best representative of
the fruition of the Mahayana path can be found in the person of
the Dalai Lama, whose unaffected compassion has touched the
hearts of millions of people. Even though Tibetan Buddhists regard
him as a manifestation of Avalokiteshvara, the bodhisattva of compassion, His Holiness emphasizes over and over again that he is just

a "simple Buddhist monk" whose "modest" realizations come from the very meditations we outlined in chapter 3.

Again, anyone who has lived in a Zen community knows that the body-mind can fall away through the practice of zazen and working with koans. A number of honest and unembellished autobiographies by Western Zen students have appeared in recent years, documenting the induction of *satori* and *kensho* experiences through intense Zen practice.[1]

Tantra, similarly, cannot be dismissed out of hand. The aim of Tantra, as we explained earlier, is to enhance and expand the energy-dynamic of our public identity through creative visualization and the control of subtle inner energies. In fact, one of the explicit intentions of Tantric practice is to create an energy field that magnetically draws people into the orbit of one's enlightened activity. And this is precisely reflected in the larger-than-life personalities of the Tantric masters who have become well known in the West— figures like Chögyam Trungpa, Thubten Yeshe, Sogyal Rinpoche, Dingo Khyentse Rinpoche, Namkhai Norbu Rinpoche, His Holiness the 16th Karmapa and others—who shift people's state of consciousness through the sheer power of the wisdom-energy they exude. At the very minimum, Tantric practice gives Westerners a much more empowered and positive outlook on life. To deny these benefits is naïve and short-sighted, if not intellectually dishonest.

Yet, when we look into the unorthodox systems, we discover that they are highly critical of the orthodox approaches to spiritual development, even going so far as to claim that they have no ultimate spiritual value whatsoever. In this chapter, we will lay out their claims and examine the logic behind them.

●　　●　　●

Dzogchen is not unique in its condemnation of the orthodox approach, for similar strictures are known, for example, in Zen and Mahamudra.[2] In these traditions we find the claim that practices such as mindfulness meditation, insight riddles, and deconstructive meditation are hindrances to the emergence of real spiritual understanding. Comparable views can be found, for example, in the

Sahajayana tradition of medieval India, as well as in certain heterodox forms of Jainism and other non-Buddhist teachings. Thus,
Saraha says:

> *If by nakedness one is released,*
> *Then dogs and jackals must be so.*
> *If from the absence of hair there comes perfection,*
> *Then the hips of the maidens must be so.*[3]

Saraha's criticism here is directed at both the Jains, certain sects of
whom went naked, and at Buddhist monks, who shave their
heads—such merely formal practices, Saraha says, are futile.

Later in the same verse, Saraha inveighs against both Mahayana
and Tantric practitioners:

> *With such investigations they fall from the Way;*
> *Some would envisage it as space,*
> *Others endow it with the nature of voidness,*
> *And thus they are generally in disagreement.*
>
> *Whoever, deprived of the Innate, seeks nirvana,*
> *Can in no wise acquire the absolute truth . . .*
>
> *Abandon such false attachments and renounce such illusion!*
> *Than knowledge of This there is nothing else.*
> *Other than This no one can know.*[4]

Again, in the Tamil Siddha tradition of South India, we find the
poet Akappey Chittar writing:

> *Mantras do not exist*
> *Experience does not exist*
> *Tantras do not exist*
> *Doctrines have been destroyed*
>
> *Rites are just devil's play*
> *Knowledge—a hollow stable*

The Lord is but an illusion
Everything is like that[5]

In exploring this topic, however, we will continue to focus on the Dzogchen tradition, although we will also draw on the teachings of Zen masters, as well as some observations made by contemporary non-aligned spiritual teachers whose roots lie in the Hindu tradition.

We will base this chapter on a particularly forthright text written by the 14th-century Tibetan master, Longchenpa. Longchenpa is regarded as the greatest scholar-yogi within the Nyingma tradition, whence whatever he has to say deserves serious attention. The sections come from a text I have referred to earlier titled *The Natural Freedom of Being*.[6] This one short text seems to capture all the arguments against goal-oriented forms of spiritual practice.

THE FUTILITY OF SPIRITUAL PRACTICE

Longchenpa begins his critique, stating that:

> Even though one may take sides and give allegiance to a philosophical system, or even [cultivate] the innumerable types of philosophical viewpoints, meditational methods or [traditions of] action, still it is difficult to see the authentic meaning of the quintessential mind itself. The disciples [of the fully awakened teachers], those who have awakened by themselves,[7] the Phenomenalists and the Dogmatic followers of Madhyamaka have gone astray through their analyses of the selflessness of the person and entities, and [by engaging] in the four actual practices of view, meditation, action and the space[-like meditation on openness], etc. It appears as though innumerable creatures [i.e. new samsaric embodiments] are created [by engaging in these techniques].[8]

Longchenpa here mentions a number of theories basic to Buddhism, such as openness of reality (*shunyata*) and the teaching that we possess no solid core of identity, and points to the futility of pursuing these as means to spiritual attainment. According to Longchenpa, it is impossible to understand the mind itself by relying on any of the philosophical systems or meditative methods that have been developed in Buddhism. By the "mind itself," Longchenpa means the mind as distinct from mental activities such as thinking and perceiving. Mind itself is unconditioned and unstained by thought activity. It is likened to a mirror that reflects the world just-as-it-is, without preferring any percept over another.

From the large range of Buddhist philosophical systems, Longchenpa specifically targets the Phenomenalists (Chittamatra or Yogachara), who held the view that all phenomena are mental; and what he calls the "Dogmatic followers of Madhyamaka." The latter are the philosophers we discussed earlier, such as Nagarjuna, Chandrakirti, and Shantideva. According to Longchenpa, meditators are actually led astray by just those deconstructive meditations that followers of Madhyamaka claim can reverse conceptuality.

Powerful exponents (*mahasiddhas*) of the Mahamudra voiced identical assessments of the negative value of traditional spiritual methods; Saraha boldly proclaimed that: "Mantras and Tantras, meditation and concentration are all a cause of self-deception. Do not defile in contemplation thought that is pure in its own nature, but abide in the bliss of yourself and cease these torments."[9]

In Zen, too, we can find similar declarations. The eighth-century Chinese master Mazu, for example, remarks: "To grasp the good and reject the bad, to contemplate emptiness and enter concentration, is all in the province of contrivance—and if you go on seeking externals, you get further and further estranged."[10] Similarly, Yuanwu, a Chinese master from the East Mountain School of Zen, wrote that, "To study Zen conceptually is like drilling in ice for fire, like digging a hole to look for the sky. It just increases mental fatigue. To study Zen by training is adding mud to dirt, scattering sand in the eyes, impeding you more and more."[11]

Longchenpa continues:

Some say that the purification of the mind is the goal of view, meditation and action. Some try to suppress their drives and feelings. Some decide to fuse these practices with the temporal [world] by claiming that our [ordinary] immediate, empirical cognition is the open [or immaterial] state! Others count the arisings and ceasings [i.e., the inhalations and exhalations of the breath]. They say these are the authentic aim [of practice, but here there are only] turbulent waves of proliferating conceptualization.[12]

Here Longchenpa singles out further meditation methods for criticism.[13] He mentions meditations designed to produce a trance-like experience and even the time-honored method of attending to the cycle of breathing, an important part of mindfulness meditation, which I discussed in chapter 2. He also notes that the suppression of emotions precipitates rather than attenuates conceptual activity. Longchenpa also criticizes those who claim that our ordinary, everyday way of experiencing the world is the open dimension that spiritual seekers desire.

He continues:

In exactly the same way, they say that the control of one's inner energies through [the practice of physical] coupling [i.e. the use of karma-mudra] in order to [generate) bliss and lucidity is the actual purpose [of practice, but in fact] they become trapped by their libidinous fixations. Through these choices, they get stuck in the net of what is acceptable and unacceptable. These people will never see the quintessential meaning. For them there is no possibility or opportunity to be liberated, and they remain trapped in the empirical world because in every case they are deluded by an intellectual construction.[14]

Longchenpa now targets some of the most elevated practices in the Tantric tradition. Recall that in Tantra, meditators attempt to control the energies in their nervous system by visualizing a network of metaphysiological channels (*nadi*) and vital energies (*prana*), which give vitality to the body and provide a subtle physical basis for emotional, mental, and spiritual processes. By controlling the flow of the energies within the channels, meditators attempt to control their conceptualizing activity. In the Tantric tradition, advanced meditators may also use sexual intercourse as a yogic practice, in conjunction with visualization and control of the vital energies, in order to produce experiences of pure bliss. The principle involved here is that an experience of bliss is the best foundation upon which to realize the lucid or clear-light nature of reality, since there is no emotional objection or resistance to what one is experiencing. However, according to Longchenpa, such practices merely stimulate emotional entanglement.

These practices stand in contrast to the highly regulated and disciplined behavior of monastics, which, as we noted earlier, is regulated by a detailed set of precepts stipulating how they are to behave in private, in public, and within monasteries and nunneries. The intention behind these behavior controls is to filter out intense feelings of desire and aversion, and thereby facilitate the practice of meditation. However, according to the Dzogchen tradition, this too represents an extreme, because monks and nuns become trapped by the numerous rules they are required to observe and lose sight of the spontaneously-arising and ever-present capacity to realize their natural state.

Longchenpa continues:

> Alas! Because these people do not recognize the precious jewel, they appear to be searching for junk jewelry, having discarded the wish-fulfilling gem. Having rejected what is impeccable, the veritable nature of the mind itself, [and instead] conditioning themselves with fabricated techniques [based on] hope and fear, they are thrown into a nest of snakes. One can never become free with an obsessed mind. The defect lies in the seeker who seeks for the meaning of that which is sought after.[15]

Having emphasized how seriously misguided these practices are,

Longchenpa comes to the heart of the problem. The assumption common to all these methods of spiritual practice is that our present condition is inadequate or impoverished, and that it shouldn't be this way. All these methods are predicated on the belief that something is missing—this isn't it. Thus, in Theravada, for example, we lack the experience of egolessness. In Zen, we lack the breakthrough illumination of *satori*. In Madhyamaka, we lack the insight that corrects our fundamental ignorance. In Tantra, we fail to live in a pure spiritual universe. The methods of these traditions are all designed to bring forth whatever is thought to be missing. Because the assumption that something is missing is so pervasive and constant, Longchenpa refers to it as the "obsessed mind."

Seeking and Never Finding

The futility of such practices is inherent in the identity of the "seeker," driven by the belief that there is something of value to be found. Yet as long as the practitioner is a seeker, she or he is doomed to be dissatisfied, since she or he has not reached the goal that is sought. Hence, Longchenpa writes that "the defect lies in the seeker who seeks for the meaning of that which is sought after."

Centuries earlier, Saraha stressed the same point—that reality is present and available, yet elusive if deliberately sought: "The nature of the sky is originally clear, but by gazing and gazing the sight becomes obscured. Then when the sky appears deformed in this way, the fool does not know that this is the fault of his own mind."[16] The ninth-century Chinese Zen master Linji makes the same observation: "when you look for it [enlightenment] you become further from it, when you seek it you turn from it all the more."[17] Longchenpa continues:

Oh! If one wants to apprehend the meaning of the nature of the mind itself, what is the use of many investigations and analyses? Whatever appears is right there, but there is no grasper of the appearance. When one has no fixations and doesn't take sides or adopt a position, one does not need to accept or reject [anything at all]. Because everything is unsteady, unalloyed and contaminated, don't mess with them![18]

The Madhyamaka claim that conceptuality can be deconstructed through analysis is a myth, according to Longchenpa. The Madhyamaka practitioner who uses the Diamond Cutter routine and the Zen practitioner who works with a koan are simply living in hope if they believe that these methods can precipitate a non-conceptual experience of reality.

"Tool" Zen

Longchenpa is joined here by some Zen masters who openly reject the use of koans for achieving *satori*. The 17th-century Japanese master Bankei, for example, rejected both sitting meditation (*zazen*) and koan practice, which he called "tool Zen":

> Zen masters of today generally use "old tools" when they deal with pupils, apparently thinking they cannot raise the barriers [to enlightenment] without them. They do not teach by thrusting themselves directly forward and confronting their students without their tools. These men who teach with tools and cannot do without them are the blind men of Zen. What is more, they tell their students that there can be no progress in Zen unless they raise a "great ball of doubt," and then break through this doubt. So, first of all, they have them raise a ball of doubt by any means possible; they do not teach them to live by the unborn Buddha-mind. Those who have no ball of doubt themselves, they saddle with one, causing them to change their Buddha-mind into a ball of doubt. That is a mistake.[19]

Bankei explains the fallacy of using methods such as koans:

> Cutting off occurring thoughts is like washing blood off in blood. The original blood might be washed off, but you're still defiled by the blood you wash in. You can wash it as much as you like, the bloodstains won't go away. You don't know that

your mind is originally unborn and undying, that it is free of illusion, and you think that thoughts really exist, so you revolve in the cycle of birth and death. You must realize that thoughts are temporary, changing appearances, and neither seize on them or hate them, just let them occur and cease of themselves. It's like the image reflected in a mirror. The mirror is clear and bright and reflects whatever is placed before it. But the image does not stay in the mirror . . . [20]

Similarly, the contemporary non-aligned teacher U. G. Krishnamurti is an outspoken critic of all forms of spiritual and religious practice.[21] According to his view:

If you practice any system of mind control, automatically the "you" is there, and through this it is continuing. . . . Nor can you practice mindfulness, trying to be aware every moment of your life. You cannot be aware; you and awareness cannot coexist. If you could be in a state of awareness for one second by the clock, once in your life, the continuity would be snapped, the illusion of the experiencing structure, the "you," would collapse, and everything would fall into the natural rhythm. In this state you do not know what you are looking at—that *is* awareness.[22]

The reason why we can't reverse the thinking process is that thought only moves in the direction of producing more thought. Hence, according to Krishnamurti, if a reversal of the thinking process is ever to occur, it must be acausal, since every attempt to cause it to stop only guarantees its continuation. It is impossible to willfully stop thinking, since every effort to do this only adds momentum to conceptual activity. In other words, we cannot *think* our way to the end of thought. He explains:

We are all talking of thought. Is it possible for you to look at thought? No, there is another thought which is looking—that is the tricky part, you see—it divides itself into two—otherwise you can't look at thought. . . . So, what creates the division? The division is created by thought—that is the beginning of your thinking. It is a very tricky process. It is one movement, and what is looking at what you call "thought" is all the definitions you have of thought. . . . So all the tricks you are playing—that if you look more carefully, with total attention . . . —all this is only deception, because all you are doing is clarifying your thinking. . . .[23]

Under this interpretation, all spiritual theories and methods, contrary to their stated aim, are absolutely guaranteed to perpetuate the practitioner's independence and individuality. It doesn't matter whether we are controlling our thoughts or letting them be, intensifying our emotions or releasing them, since all the experiences that arise are appropriated by the ego—the ego designs progressively more sophisticated methods for disguising its commitment to self-maintenance. The most sophisticated methods are found in the domain of spirituality, where the name of the game is to "transcend the self." Thus, within the domain of spirituality we find a number of inventions that are designed to disguise our finite and ego-based existence. We have notions such as "timelessness," "non-conceptuality," and "non-self," which all act to maintain the status quo.

For example, the continuation of time is guaranteed by inventing the concept of a "timeless dimension" and then pursuing an experience of "the timeless." In similar fashion, thought creates the possibility of a state of "no-thought" and then ensures its own maintenance for as long as no-thought is sought. At a conceptual level, postulates such as the "timeless dimension" can only be defined as pairs of opposites: in the absence of the idea of time, there can be no idea of timelessness. In other words, it is the very concept of time which itself provides the scope for postulating a timeless realm, and each of these concepts defines and perpetuates the other. Similarly, no-thought exists in binary opposition to thought. The pursuit of the experience of no-thought thus ensures the perpetuation of thought. In each case, what seemed to be promising turns out to be a vicious circle.

GRADUAL VERSUS SUDDEN ENLIGHTENMENT

The points made by these and other Zen and Dzogchen masters may seem to be rather arcane, but they are at the heart of a debate that has occupied Buddhist practitioners for centuries. The issues that we grapple with in terms of trying to discover how best to relieve our suffering and confusion are precisely those that have pre-occupied all seekers.

Zen Buddhists, for example, have been cued in right from the beginning to the question of whether a conditioned practice can lead to the experience of no-mind (*wu-hsin*).[24] The two different responses to this question produced a division between those who argued that enlightenment was attained gradually (*chien-wu*) and those who said it was an instantaneous event (*tun-wu*).

According to records recovered from the cave libraries of Tun-huang, a "Southern Line" of Chinese Ch'an was established in the eighth century by Ho-tse Shen-hui, who wanted to distinguish his approach from his "Northern Line" contemporaries, who advocated a graduated approach to awakening.[25] The Northern Line empha-sized practices aimed at purifying the mind of adventitious defile-ments in order to clear the way for a direct apprehension of origi-nal awakening (*pen-wu*). This was the standard Ch'an position up until the middle of the eighth century.[26]

Inspired by the awakening of his own teacher Hui-neng—who taught that "the very passions are themselves enlightenment (*bodhi*)"[27]—Ho-tse Shen-hui developed a more radical position based on the immediate recognition of the mind-nature. Ho-tse Shen-hui argued that the Northern Line's approach was based on the notion of "gradual practice" (*chien-hsiu*), because it emphasized mental purity. Implicit in this is an assumption that the undefiled mind-nature is separate from defilement. This assumption perpet-uates a subtle form of dualism that associates purity with meditative quiescence, and regards this as superior to normal consciousness. According to Ho-tse Shen-hui, this practice keeps the meditator trapped within *samsara*, because it encourages attachment to a par-ticular understanding of purity. Ho-tse Shen-hui characterized the

Northern Line approach as "doing something" (*yu-tso*) and his own approach as "doing nothing" (*wu-tso*).

During the eighth century, there emerged in Ch'an an even more radical movement, associated with Ma-tsu. Earlier schools, such as those promoted by Ho-tse and Niu-t'ou, held that there is a pure mind-nature that is obscured by deluded thoughts, even though these have no substantial reality. Ma-tsu went further and argued that the deluded thoughts are in fact a manifestation of the buddha-nature. For Ma-tsu nothing needs to be cultivated or removed from the mind, for everything is already perfect.[28] According to Kuei-feng Tsung-mi, the Hung-chou school of Ma-Tsu taught that:

> The path is the mind; you cannot use the mind to cultivate the mind. Evil too is the mind; you cannot use the mind to excise the mind. One who neither excises evil nor cultivates good, one who is completely free and spontaneous in all situations: this is called a liberated man. There is no dharma which can bind, no Buddha which can be produced. The mind is like space which can be neither supplemented nor diminished. How can we presume to supplement it? And why is this? There is not one dharma which can be found outside the mind nature; hence cultivation means simply to allow the mind to act spontaneously.[29]

The Deception of "Selflessness"

One of the most sophisticated ways of perpetuating the ego is found in the Buddhist theory of egolessness, which we discussed earlier. This theory holds that we possess no solid core or defining characteristics; thus within this theory, the ego denies its own existence, and thereby creates the ideal and goal of realizing egolessness as a way of sealing the ongoing existence of the ego. The game plan of the ego goes undetected in this theory, because the ego is merely an illusion.

The Dzogchen tradition, on the other hand, contrasts the mind that obsessively seeks to maintain its existence with the natural mind, which simply allows whatever is there to be there, without fixation or preference. This mind doesn't seek to determine whether what one is experiencing should or shouldn't be there. It doesn't accept some aspects of experience and reject others. It simply allows what is present to be present just-as-it-is, without bias or fixation.

Longchenpa states:

> If these objects which appear to the mind exist in the mode of openness, then what need is there to search for their openness? [On the other hand] if [appearances] do not exist [in the mode of openness], then even though one searches [for their openness] they cannot become open or empty. Therefore, what is the use of [engaging] in this meaningless and arduous task [of actively seeking the open or empty dimension of appearances].[30]

In order to drive home the futility of meditating on openness, Longchenpa reasons that if objects are empty to begin with—that is, if they lack an intrinsic existence—then it is the case that they indeed *are* empty. Why go searching for something that already is? It would be like searching for your foot when you're already standing on it. On the other hand, if things aren't empty of intrinsic or inherent characteristics, then no amount of searching will discover their openness. Saraha says much the same thing: "If it's already manifest, what's the use of meditation? And if it is hidden, one is just measuring darkness."[31]

Trying Is Hopeless

Longchenpa makes the further point that exerting oneself to achieve an understanding of the ultimate reality effectively places the ultimate beyond one's experience. It doesn't matter if this is an all-out struggle to achieve spiritual awakening, or just a gentle change in one's perspective designed to cultivate a more accurate perception of reality. The very notion of exertion implies that one is trying to achieve or gain something one doesn't already have; and according to Dzogchen, one cannot have more or less of what one already has, since this would mean that things can be different from the way they are. The 14th-century Zen master Yuansou explains this well: "In Buddhism there is no place to apply effort. Everything in it is normal—you put on clothes to keep warm and eat food to stop hunger—that's all. If you consciously try to think about it, it is not what you think of. If you consciously try to arrange it, it is not what you arrange."[32]

Ying-an, a master from the East Mountain School of Zen, makes a similar point: "If you have a single thought of eagerness to attain Zen mastery, this burns out your potential, so you cannot grow anymore."[33]

The contemporary Indian teacher H. W. L. Poonja connects the application of effort with the creation of time: "If you make any effort or use any method of trying to achieve something at some distant future, this will bring you into time. And time is mind. So this will be the play of mind only. But your original nature is empty."[34]

Longchenpa continues:

> [Ultimately] there are no mantras, no Tantras and there are no final philosophical positions. [Reality] cannot be identified as "this" or "that," and there is no view, meditation, enactment or fruition of these. Everything that exists is in a state of perfect harmony in the form of a single mandala. Philosophical systems, view, meditation, enactment and fruition are [all] fulfilled. Cyclic existence (*samsara*) and the state of unconditioned freedom (*nirvana*) are equally fulfilled and (the sphere of) reality itself (*dharmata*) has thus become all pervading.[35]

At this point, Longchenpa begins to contrast the state of being that is naturally attuned to the way things are, with the spiritual life that is lived in the conscious and deliberate pursuit of a goal such as enlightenment or nirvana. From the perspective of Dzogchen, nirvana is no more intrinsically preferable than samsara. Bondage and liberation are co-emergent and interdependent, and consequently lack any real existence and are already intrinsically free.

Longchenpa continues:

> Alas! For one whose mind is fixated with biased attitudes,
> there is no possibility of freedom. The factor which binds one
> is just these biased attitudes. As long as one is to be free of
> opinions and fixed extremes, there is no other way of depict-
> ing [the state of unbiased freedom]. One cannot see it by
> looking for it. Nor can one find it through logical analysis.
> [The nature of reality] cannot be depicted as "this" or "that,"
> but it presents itself in a very ordinary way, and so you should
> not use your mind of attachment as a means of liberation.[36]

In this section, Longchenpa makes the point that one cannot see
reality by looking for it. There is no need to look for it, because it is
already there—wherever one is. As he says, "it presents itself in a very
ordinary way." In fact, the very act of looking blinds one, because it
implies that one needs to be doing something in order to see it.
Longchenpa continues:

> Although people desire the non-dualistic and limitless
> [awareness, they make a] limit out of that which is not limited
> [and thereby] constrict the quintessential mind itself. Even
> though people desire [the realization of] both [the ultimate
> and relative] realities, they fall into an extreme [understand-
> ing of the two realities]. Although people desire the union of
> opposites, this is not the way things naturally work. No mat-
> ter in what way conceptual constructions [are imposed], one
> is trapped in the cage of [conflicting] desires.[37]

That is, the very act of trying to escape what one is experiencing
keeps one caught in a structure that perpetually oscillates between
the poles of desire and aversion. Thus, according to Longchenpa,
desire—even the desire for a laudable spiritual objective, such as
harmonizing conflicting emotions or the integration of the spiritual
and everyday realities—limits people's understanding of reality,
since the quintessential mind is not something that can be desired.

In other words, what one desires is an image or fantasy about the quintessential mind—it is not the quintessential mind itself. Similarly, H. W. L. Poonja asks: "When you run to the idea to meditate for freedom, where are you standing? In bondage or not? Do you not have an idea in the mind that you wish to be free from something? So you sit in bondage. You are meditating on bondage, not freedom!"[38]

Longchenpa reiterates the negative effects of earnest and well-intentioned spiritual practice:

From the very beginning, we have been burdened by the illusion of objects of perception and one who perceives. And even now when we investigate with great urgency, we are trapped by mental images. Alas! I feel pity for the deluded mind.[39]

Here, Longchenpa continues the theme that one should not become fixated on how things are:

If one identifies [the mind itself] as being "this" or "that" [i.e., identifies it as some particular thing] then this is not the view [to take]. One does not need the cage of proliferating conceptualization. In [the field of] bare awareness [*vidya*], whatever [appearances] arise [in one's mind), they cannot be counted or enumerated, and thus one must not [consider some states of consciousness] to be expanded and others contracted, or some sublime and others profane. Thus, one should give up one's libidinous fixations.

With respect to the appearances in the mind, there is a freedom from the mental orientation [that thinks] "It is this." Do not condition [your mind by trying] to suppress [your experience], grasp it or [otherwise] contaminate it, but let [your mind] rest naturally in whatever [condition you find it]. This is the incontrovertible quintessence of what is ultimately meaningful.[40]

Attempting to condition the mind by either suppressing experience or grasping at it merely obscures the mind's natural state, and produces confusion. One should instead allow the mind to rest in its natural state, without doing anything to it whatsoever or interfering with it in any way. In the Dzogchen tradition, this is known as "liberating the mind into its own nature." Garab Dorje, regarded as the first teacher of the Dzogchen tradition, explains:

> Whatever may arise or appear [as external phenomena], is merely one's own state of existence [that manifests]. Apart from this organized and structured system of phenomena, which [in fact] does not exist [in reality], one can obtain nothing. By virtue of the totality of its inherent . . . power . . . [awareness] allows various different kinds of phenomena to liberate [of themselves], and, therefore, there exists no other antidote.[41]

Non-fixation applies equally to the mundane and the sublime. In fact, the very distinction between the ordinary and the spiritual only serves to trap one, since it can lead one into believing that one has understood or comprehended what the spiritual search is all about. But, as Foyan, a master from the East Mountain School of Zen says, "The minute you fixate on the recognition that 'This is it,' you are immediately bound hand and foot and cannot move around anymore."[42]

Longchenpa continues:

> All the varieties of entities are actually in a state of equanimity. Whatever [thoughts] arise they are devoid of duality, and so they are the transcendental wisdom [*ye shes*]. Do not intellectually conceptualize it or search for it with your egocentric mind! Do not be trapped by the objects of perception, and do not [let your mind] become tarnished by [functioning as a] subject of cognitions. One should know that all the entities that exist are like space. If [all phenomena should be] seen to be equal [in the same way that] magical illusions [are of equal value and worth in virtue of being illusory], and if there are

no objects of desire, then not [believing in the] natural duality [of things] is the supreme king of views. The real test or
measure [of oneself] is the realization of an unlimited and
nonperipheral [awareness]. How wonderful![43]

OUR PRACTICE IS ALREADY FULFILLED

According to Dzogchen, there is no distinction between appearance
and reality, or between confusion and wisdom. There isn't anything
"other" than what is present for a person in any moment. There is
no such thing as an "obstruction" or "hindrance" to enlightenment,
for this presupposes that one experience can displace another.
Hence, Longchenpa claims that thoughts *are* the nondual and non-
conceptual wisdom, and similarly, that phenomena *are* the very
medium that they displace.

The test of one's realization, then, is one's capacity to see and
experience the transcendental field of being as indistinguishable
from the sense-world as it manifests each moment. In fact, it is misleading to talk in terms of finding the two indistinguishable, for it
isn't a question of infusing sense experience with the effective qualities of supersensory spiritual experiences.

Spiritual goals such as enlightenment are a full-scale distraction
from being just-as-one-is. Enlightenment becomes a possibility the
instant one declares that human existence is limited or unsatisfactory. And for as long as one seeks to escape from that which is now
unsatisfactory, human existence continues to be limited and
painful. Complete fulfillment is forsaken the moment one buys into
the "myth of spiritual liberation." Hence, Longchenpa continues:

There is no need to discard [some experiences] and cultivate
[others]. [Whether one's experiences] are dynamic or stable,
one should let them go wherever they want to go. Dynamic
and stable [experiences], tranquillity (*shamatha*) and discernment (*vipashyana*), and skillful means (*upaya*) and transcendental knowledge are all united. Do not condition this [bare
awareness] by intellectualizations and do not manipulate and

mechanize your experiences. If there [are views and opinions] to be negated and established, and [things that need] to be rejected and accepted, then in the process of doing that, one gets entangled in the web of dualistic fixations [which are based on] hope and fear. Having failed to arrive at the place one wants to go, one is thrown into a state of estrangement. Therefore, no matter what [one experiences], one should cultivate non-acceptance and non-rejection as the point or purpose [of one's practice].[44]

Here Longchenpa emphasizes the non-strategic nature of Dzogchen as a life wherein we allow our experiences to take their own course. Philosophical argument and technical meditation have no place here, since they only serve to consolidate the belief that we should be where other people are, or others should be where we are ourselves. The names reserved for people who are where we want to be are "buddhas" and "bodhisattvas." Those who should be where we are ourselves are the confused and unenlightened. The exercise, then, is to leave things as they are—neither accepting nor rejecting whatever we experience. In this way, we are completely fulfilled.

Longchenpa concludes the section we have been discussing:

Friends! The mind is like an ignorant camel. If one holds onto it, [it wants to] escape, but if one lets it loose, it just sits there. If one relaxes into one's natural state, this is the veritable state of natural freedom.[45] Then by naturally releasing [the mind] into its own condition, [beyond the fixations] of cognitions and a cognizer, one discovers the blissful quality of one's mind. Therefore, one should let go of the mind that is deliberately attentive and stay [in the state that is] free of deliberate attentiveness, in which there is no conditioning and tarnishing of whatever arises [in one's experience]. Then, free from the duality of cognitions and a cognizer, one remains in a state of totally natural freedom, and unhindered, one's awareness, lucidity and openness radiate.[46]

7

The Edge
of Certainty

We are now in a position to formulate the dilemma implicit in the preceding chapters. On the one hand, there stand what we have called the orthodox traditions of Buddhism, which teach meditation and other forms of spiritual practice, and provide the circumstances for such practices through the creation of monasteries, temples, and centers. On the other hand, we find highly accomplished masters from respected Buddhist traditions declaring that orthodox methods for spiritual advancement are useless.

At a philosophical level, the contrast is between systems which in one way or another say that spiritual practice can causally produce a non-conceptual awareness, and those which claim that practice can never be an agent for the emergence of spiritual insight. Thus Madhyamaka, for example, claims that the liberating insight into openness arises in dependence on deconstructive analysis. It rejects the proposition that insight occurs adventitiously or through no cause at all. Dzogchen practitioners, by contrast, claim that spiritual methods perpetuate conceptualization and do not give rise to spiritual insight.

Spiritual seekers relate to these philosophical positions personally as conflicting beliefs and attitudes that accompany the spiritual endeavor. These are experienced as feelings and orientations that can change from year to year and day to day, and can be summarized thus:

• There is something to do	• There is nothing to do
• This isn't it	• This is it
• There is something to get	• There isn't anything to get
• There is something I need to know	• There is nothing I need to know
• I need to think about this more	• Thinking won't help me
• I must hang on	• I should just let go
• I need to stop thinking	• Thinking and not-thinking are irrelevant
• I need help	• I don't need help
• I need to exercise care	• I'll be carefree
• I'll persevere	• I'll give up striving
• This is meaningful	• This is meaningless

Broadly, the attitudes on the left signify the orientation of the orthodox traditions, while those on the right are closer to the perspective of the unorthodox traditions.[1]

•   •   •

Before proceeding further, it may be useful to orient ourselves in terms of our own preference *vis-à-vis* the orthodox and unorthodox interpretations of the value of spiritual practice. In general terms, we are either resolved or unresolved about this question. We can become resolved in two ways. One possibility is that we have taken a position in favor of the orthodox or the unorthodox interpretation. The position we have adopted might be consistent with how we have thought about this question in the past, or it could represent a change in our thinking. Again, we might have achieved a point of resolution by settling into the position that there is no right interpretation, or that it is impossible to decide which approach is correct. In this stance, we are certain that the problem is insoluble in terms of a simple decision in favor of one or the other interpretation.

If we are unable to come down unequivocally on either side, or are uncomfortable with declaring that the dilemma simply can't be resolved, we are in a state of irresolution. In other words, we don't know where we are—we have lost our bearings and can't respond decisively to the question of where we are situated *vis-à-vis* the correctness or adequacy of the orthodox versus the unorthodox interpretation of the spiritual endeavor.

With respect to the state of resolution, we should note that in validating one interpretation and invalidating the other we have settled into a philosophical position. By agreeing with either the orthodox or unorthodox interpretation, we adopt a viewpoint and thereby forsake the "positionless position" of Zen, Madhyamaka, and the unorthodox schools, for strictly speaking, these schools would neither defend nor refute anything as representing their own philosophy. By aligning ourselves with either interpretation, we ignore a common guiding vision, which is to be free of any viewpoint. Both acceptance and rejection represent an intellectual resolution of problems, but Madhyamaka, Zen, and Dzogchen close off such a conceptual resolution because it has no spiritual value.

RETRACING OUR STEPS

At this point, it might be instructive to pause and consider why you are persevering with this book and the dilemma it is seeking to expose, for the answer to that question may have something to say about how you live the spiritual life.

We have suggested that the practice of Buddhism can be problematic in a number of ways, and herein lies the first clue to what has transpired. The claim that the spiritual life is problematic has a particularly seductive pull to it, for we are willing consumers of the story that spiritual practice is demanding and difficult. We are also very prone to subscribe to the belief that the dynamics of spiritual evolution can be subtle and mysterious. Consequently, in many of the traditions we have mentioned, it is necessary to commit oneself to a rigorous discipline and consult a teacher if one is to successfully negotiate the spiritual path.

Moreover, the fact that this discussion appears in the form of a book purporting to deal with Buddhism adds in a sense to the difficulty, since such books typically tackle "real" problems and work toward furthering our understanding of the issues, if not toward resolving them altogether. As a reader of this book you are, at least to some extent, already predisposed to accept the suggestion that there are conflicting approaches to living the spiritual life. You are ready to bite into any "deep issue" surrounding spiritual activities.

In other words, we have structured our discussion thus far to some extent—at least implicitly—as a "problem" for which we are seeking a "solution." In accepting this structure, we have done what we always do. We create a problem—be it conceptual, personal, or spiritual—and then set about trying to find a solution for it. The earnestness and sincerity with which we read our spiritual source books (or even this book) highlight the fact that the problem I have constructed in this book is our problem. It makes no difference whether you agree or disagree with how I have described or analyzed the problem, or whether you agree or disagree with specific positions within our framework of discussion, since they all point to the fact that we are searching for understanding and some degree of certainty.

So how did we construct this problem? Our first step was simply to declare that the role and function of spiritual practice is problematic and often ambiguous. We then personalized the problem by suggesting that earnest spiritual seekers quite legitimately and appropriately find themselves wondering from time to time whether the best or most profitable spiritual activity is to do their *sadhana*—their insight meditation, *zazen,* koan practice, and so forth—or to transform their regular activities into a spiritual activity by adding the "right" type of attitude or motivation; or just to do what they are doing, without any concern at all about whether it is or isn't a spiritual activity. We went on to suggest that two important sets of traditions—the orthodox and unorthodox—have something of interest and value to say about the role of spiritual practice. The high regard in which the representative traditions are held helped to trigger the assessment that we were dealing with a real and important issue, even though this flies in the face of their assertion that they have nothing to defend. In other words, we come to a book about Zen, and we read that Zen maintains that there is nothing to achieve, and that the point of spiritual practice is to realize this. We thus take on board the paradoxes that these statements enclose and use them to create an issue: If what Zen says is true, how are we to realize that there is nothing to realize?

Having distinguished the orthodox and unorthodox approaches to spirituality, we then suggested that their positions were different. Indeed, we said that they contradict each other. Having juxtaposed these conflicting positions, we then invited, you, the reader, into our dilemma. And as any clear thinker knows, a dilemma is constricting and binding. A dilemma paralyzes one. If we are stuck on the horns of a dilemma, we cannot move easily and naturally—it is uncomfortable, to say the least. Having set the stage, we invited you into the important task of seeking a solution to a very real problem. This need, it seems reasonable to suggest, has provided you with the motivation for persevering with this book up to now.

Having seen why we are still persevering with this journey, the options at this point are clearly either to give up, or continue. And either step will disclose our orientation. If we continue, this points to an orthodox interpretation of spirituality that sees us as constrained or trapped in some way, and in need of some insight to liberate us from our predicament. If we give up, on the other hand, we have aligned ourselves with the unorthodox perspective that sees the problem either as a total fabrication, or of no spiritual value in pursuing.

A MIDDLE-PATH RESOLUTION

Given that you have decided to continue on our journey together, we now need to discover some means of working toward increased clarity and resolution.

Were Nagarjuna privy to our present deliberations (or confusions), he would invite us to clarify our thinking about how spiritual methods and spiritual insight are related. He would invite us to uncover our beliefs: both the beliefs we might have acquired through our study and spiritual practices, and our innate beliefs about the spiritual enterprise. So what positions are explicit or implied in the story we have developed?

To summarize, generally speaking, the orthodox interpretation is that spiritual insight is a product of diligently applying spiritual methods; while the unorthodox interpretation says that spiritual practice is unrelated to spiritual insight. These theories, of course, are mutually exclusive.

The Madhyamaka approach, as we explained earlier, is to resolve theories into two mutually excluding and jointly exhaustive hypotheses for the purpose of producing a paradox which will preclude having any valid position at all about the issue in question. In the present case, the two causal theories that serve the requirement of developing such a paradox are:

1. That spiritual insight is radically different from the spiritual methods that produce insight;

2. That the methods and the insight are co-extensive and essentially the same.

The second theory appears in Zen, for example, under the assumption that sitting in zazen is the goal, and also in some traditions of mindfulness practice where mindfulness is itself viewed as a kind of mini-enlightenment.

There is a third explanation, which may be called a "hybrid," for Madhyamaka recognizes that people often offer explanations involving the combination of two mutually-excluding positions. A hybrid explanation here is the theory that spiritual methods and spiritual insight are in some sense the same, yet also quite different. The hybrid theory is usually associated with the idea that spiritual methods mature into insight in a gradual and progressive manner. During this transition process, we can't precisely say whether the methods are the same as insight or different.

A fourth possibility that Madhyamaka considers is that insight is uncaused. Strictly, this is extending the formalities of the analysis, because it isn't a causal explanation for the arising of insight. However, in order to capture acausal theories, followers of Madhyamaka also consider this alternative.

Together, the above alternatives constitute what is known as the "four-cornered negation," which covers all possible viewpoints about whatever topic is under investigation.

In order to analyze the question further, we must apply a "template," an abstracted analytical framework superimposed on a "live" philosophical issue. The template that immediately lends itself to our needs is the "production template," which picks up on four ways in which something can come into existence, and then produces a logical paradox for each alternative. The four methods of production are:

1. Production from self

2. Production from another

3. Production from both self and another

4. Production from no cause

Using this template, a follower of Madhyamaka can logically produce a set of internal contradictions in every possible theory about how practice can be related to insight. The paradoxical deconstruction runs as follows.

1. Nothing Changes (Production from Self)

The first option is that insight is produced by insight itself. This branches into two possibilities: that spiritual practice is the same as insight; and that spiritual insight is an ever-present state that perpetuates itself indefinitely.

Dealing with the first of these possibilities, if practice is the same as spiritual insight, then meditation, koan investigation, and paradoxical deconstruction can only generate more of the same—meditation simply fuels more meditation, koan investigation stimulates further koan investigation, paradoxical analysis only ever produces the need for more deconstruction. This assumption, of course, is the basis for the critique offered by Krishnamurti and others, that thinking can only produce more thought. The absurdity here is that spiritual insight (the product) is reduced to the status of spiritual practice (the producer). Therefore, insight is the activity of wrestling with a koan, struggling to establish a visualization, or analytically searching for oneself.

The second possibility—that spiritual insight is an ever-present state that perpetuates itself indefinitely—represents an interpretation consistent with the teachings of the unorthodox traditions; nothing needs to change, since we are already enlightened. However, if insight is really born from itself, then it has always existed in a fully-fledged form. Under this interpretation, if meditation, koan inquiry, and so on aren't insight itself, then they are not a cause of insight. The absurdity here is that if spiritual methods are not identical with spiritual insight, then they are unrelated to the occurrence of spiritual insight.

2. Radical Transformation (Production from Another)

The second option is that spiritual insight is both radically different from the experience of mindfulness practice, deconstructive meditation, and so on, yet at the same time brought about through the practice of these techniques. Madhyamaka views this interpretation as an instance of "production from another," since the moment of insight has prior causes in the form of discernment meditation, but at the same time represents an experience totally different from those that preceded it. However, this interpretation suffers from the contradiction that if the moment of insight is intrinsically different from what has preceded it, then any prior mental state could equally produce insight. Getting drunk, standing on one's head, washing one's socks, taking a shower, or anything else could just as well serve as a cause—the immediately prior state becomes immaterial.

In other words, if the two states are radically discontinuous in terms of their defining characteristics, then no form of practice can foster the development of insight. Thus, any practice whatever, or no practice at all, could cause insight, which makes nonsense out of the concept of causation. Thus "production from another" reduces to "production from no cause," to which we shall turn in due course.

3. Gradual Change (Production from Self and Other)

The third option views the experience of insight as growing out of a non-insightful state of consciousness. In this interpretation, insight represents the maturation of an awareness that is latent or germinal in the normal mode of awareness. This is analogous to an acorn producing an oak tree in the presence of the right circumstances and conditions. The tree is different from the seed, yet there is a genetic continuity, for the tree emerges out of the seed. In the same way, the fully developed insight into reality is a different mode of awareness from that which precedes it, yet it emerges from within each preceding state of consciousness. This is a "commonsense" position on the question of the relationship between spiritual insight and spiritual methods.

In order to dismantle this interpretation, it is necessary to establish whether insight is an intrinsically different condition from lack of awareness. If it is intrinsically different, then Madhyamaka will maintain that this interpretation resolves into a case of "production from another." If it is not intrinsically different, then our model becomes an instance of "production from self." Either way, the interpretation can be shown to be self-contradictory.

However, this option gives us the chance to be very slippery. We can try to wriggle our way through the paradoxes by claiming that our interpretation is more complex and that it cannot be resolved into a simple case of either "production from self" or "production from another." In response to such a claim, Madhyamaka will invite us to clarify this complex process. As we clarify the process and become specific about it, our description will inevitably resolve itself into one or another of the alternatives, or cleanly segment into both, and paradoxical consequences will result.

4. Uncaused (Production from No Cause)

The fourth option is that spiritual insight simply doesn't have a cause. According to this interpretation, spiritual insight occurs as a totally unpredictable event and is unrelated to any antecedent causes or conditions whatsoever. If and when it happens, it does so spontaneously and for no apparent reason.

If we subject this interpretation to a Madhyamaka analysis, however, it resolves into a case of "production from no cause." If this is the case, it must be disqualified as a causal account for the development of spiritual insight. Activities such as meditation, koan investigation, or just "letting things be" therefore have nothing whatsoever to do with the gaining of spiritual insight.

* * *

The composite conclusion of this deconstructive analysis, therefore, is that spiritual insight doesn't arise through spiritual practice, nor does it not arise through spiritual practice.

This is all very well, but it seems that we are still left with the question of whether any real progress has been made. Progress and lack of progress, however, are assessments resting on a background of interpretation. According to Madhyamaka, deconstructing the problem is useful because it leads to a conceptual impasse. The conclusion that spiritual practice neither helps nor hinders the acquisition of spiritual insight is regarded as progressive because it blocks the possibility of adopting any fixed or definite viewpoint about this issue. The strength of the retaining barrier depends on the rigor, intentionality, depth, and focus of thought brought to bear on the analysis.

However, if we consider the matter from the viewpoint of Dzogchen, we haven't progressed at all. We have simply kept our thought active under the guise of trying to reverse the proliferation of conceptuality. Our meta-analytical exercise has thus served only to perpetuate the inquiry—it simply ran it on for another few pages. It is just "chapter two" in a never-ending saga of trying to think our way to the end of thought. In fact, if we believe that we have made progress we have gone backward, because in reality we are still at the point where we began: namely, in the middle of one thought, waiting for the next.

* * *

So where can we go from here, assuming that we still feel the need to gain some resolution of these problems?

THE ORTHODOX RESOLUTION

Under the orthodox interpretation of Buddhism, the radical differences between the orthodox and unorthodox versions of spirituality present us with a problem that is sometimes resolved through recourse to the distinction between insight (*prajna*) and method (*upaya*). In terms of this distinction, different or seemingly conflicting philosophies and systems of practice within Buddhism can be reconciled or harmonized by the notion that different spiritual perspectives are needed in order to penetrate the ultimate spiritual reality of egolessness or suchness.

According to this theory, there is no right interpretation. Every interpretation has a purpose and is validated through fulfilling that purpose. Each interpretation is like a different story, the aim of which is to awaken different listeners to the fact of who they are— their pains, accomplishments, and possibilities. For example, the purpose of the interpretation that insight involves a radical transformation (production from another) is to draw attention to the mystical and radically transforming nature of the insight into openness. The audience for this interpretation is composed of those meditators who are already accomplished in the meditative arts. This "leap" interpretation serves to highlight the unconditional nature of spiritual insight. Similarly, the purpose of the developmental interpretation (production from self and other) is to offer practitioners ongoing validation of their daily spiritual commitments. Again, the purpose behind the interpretation that we are already enlightened (production from self) is to heighten people's appreciation of the omnipresence of their natural state. And the interpretation that spiritual practice can only perpetuate itself (production from self) points to the fact that today was like yesterday and that we shouldn't be disappointed or feel cheated if tomorrow is pretty much like today—this interpretation corrects our hope that the goods will be delivered in the next meditation session.

In fact, we need look no further than Longchenpa if we wish to substantiate and validate the orthodox resolution. In the very text we used to provide the anti-method critique, Longchenpa describes, and indeed recommends, a wide range of meditative methods drawn from the Tibetan Mahayana and Tantric traditions! If we consider the text as a unit, we might conclude that he rejects the proposition that meditative tools have any ultimate value, while at the same time endorsing their capacity to produce a whole range of experiences that support and facilitate realizing the nature of reality itself.

And of course, this is precisely the understanding in mainstream Dzogchen and Mahamudra. While the unorthodox approaches acknowledge that the ultimate state of realization transcends the need for meditation or any other practice, they almost invariably invoke an orthodox understanding, stating that certain prerequisites are necessary in order to access the state of unconditioned awareness. In other words, they claim that certain conditions in the mind of a practitioner must precede awakening. Even though awakening requires no effort or understanding, the ability to relax and be receptive only comes through considerable initial effort and application. This receptiveness requires concerted meditation practice under the guidance of a qualified teacher. The contemporary Tibetan Nyingma master Chokyi Nyima Rinpoche writes that:

> Although Mahamudra is without circumstance, a qualified master is the influential circumstance for realising Mahamudra because it is through one's devotion combined with the master's oral instructions that one can recognise the natural state of mind, ground Mahamudra. Therefore, one must rely on a teacher. Realisation doesn't happen by itself.[2]

In fact, the Dzogchen and Mahamudra traditions categorize people into three groups, depending on their spiritual aptitude: the orthodox methods found in Mahayana are designed for those of inferior aptitude; the technology of Tantra is for average practitioners; and the unorthodox Dzogchen and Mahamudra approach is for superior minds. Even Hui-neng agrees: in the *Platform Scripture* he says, "Good friends, in the Dharma there is no sudden and gradual, but among people some are keen and others dull. The deluded recommend the gradual method, the enlightened practice the sudden teachings."[3]

Asked to account for the capacity of some people to instantly access the nondualistic approach, seemingly without any need for the conventional preliminaries, the unorthodox systems offer the rationale that such an aptitude derives from spiritual training in past lives. Thus, in a sense, Ch'an/Zen, Dzogchen, and Mahamudra are orthodox, to all but a few exceptionally gifted people.

· · ·

Longchenpa may thus be making an ultimately false connection between the methods of Buddhism and spiritual awakening in order to introduce his students to a level of awakening that completely transcends the need for further practice or strategic intervention. A less gratuitous explanation, however, is that the methods are merely devices that give temporary satisfaction to the illusion that there really is a path, a goal, and something to do. As the 14th-century Chinese Zen master Yuansou said, such expedient means "are all simply means of stopping children from whining."[4]

A related way to resolve the dilemma is to invoke the theory of two levels of reality.[5] Under this interpretation, the orthodox methods are valid, but only at the relative level of truth. In this case, we are invited to believe that mindfulness practice, koans, and paradoxical deconstruction are valid and effective within the fictitious world that we create as a product of our interpretations. These ultimately unnecessary practices allow us to break through the illusions of our interpretations and directly experience the ultimate reality. By contrast, the unorthodox traditions present the ultimate truth in which there is no path, no goal, and no spiritual practice.

An extension of this explanation, which accounts for contradictory philosophical frameworks, is that such frameworks arise as corrections to each other. For example, when our spiritual life is shaped by the belief that there is something to do, this is viewed as limiting, and to balance this belief, philosophers have articulated systems that advocate that we let things be as they are. Conversely, the belief that there is nothing to do at all is suitably balanced by suggestions of specific things to think or do. In this interpretation, the orthodox and unorthodox emerge in contrast to each other, as corrections to two extreme points of view. While these frameworks don't present themselves in this way, it can be argued that they are created as practitioners swing away from upholding one or the other position to the primary question of whether there is something specific they should be doing. The reasons behind such swings are usually the presence of moods such as boredom, frustration, or some other form of dissatisfaction.

This might sound useful, and this or any other explanation could undoubtedly be developed further in various interesting ways. But the real point here is that in reality, we are just constructing another orthodox interpretation of the spiritual endeavor in which methods of spiritual practice have a valued place.

Once we begin to rehearse the standard talk about these positions as heuristic devices that provide the appropriate adjustment for people at different points in their spiritual growth, we fall into the orthodox extreme. In other words, if we say that the orthodox and unorthodox are complementary approaches to the ultimate viewpoint that adheres to neither one nor the other, we fall toward the extreme of believing that we are located on a path and heading for a goal. Similarly, if we invoke the theory of two levels of reality, this signals that we have fallen to the orthodox extreme, since it presupposes that there is something to attain: namely, the ultimate viewpoint. In each of these orthodox interpretations, we are seeking a resolution to the dilemma by trying to explain our way out of it.

Of course, both the need for these explanations and the explanations themselves arise only within an orthodox orientation to spirituality. So what is the unorthodox position?

THE UNORTHODOX RESOLUTION

However plausible and satisfying these orthodox interpretations may be, they do not resolve the problem we have constructed. Moreover, such interpretations are roundly rejected by the unorthodox systems, in those sections of Dzogchen, Mahamudra, and Zen texts where this position is presented. According to the unorthodox interpretation, there is no problem to be resolved either in the spiritual life or in this book, and hence a distinction between insight and methods is unnecessary and irrelevant.

Whereas in orthodox systems, methods give rise to insight and wisdom, in the unorthodox systems there is no difference between wisdom and method. As Mañjushrimitra says, "since the state of pure and total presence of the Joyful One does not exist, it is a magical apparition of that [state] that appears to those who are deluded."[6] If sublime or ecstatic experiences occur, they occur simply because they occur. They have no significance. They aren't indicative of either enlightenment or progress, since there is nowhere to progress to and no enlightenment to attain. Experiences are experienced as what they are, as lasting for as long as they last, and as changing into whatever follows them. They occur without any theological or mystical fabrication.

Of course, we must note that if this perspective sounds attractive, then we are sliding into the unorthodox extreme in which there is nothing to do and nothing to get.

. . .

While we are now perhaps beginning to recognize how and when we are falling into either an orthodox or unorthodox extreme, we still don't know how to resolve the fundamental dilemma of two contradicting interpretations of the role and value of spiritual practice. Clearly, whether or not we take this seriously depends, in its turn, on whether our perceptions at this point are conditioned through either orthodox or unorthodox eyes.

If we are still intent on persevering with this problem, then we are located within an orthodox framework, "the discourse of change," as we have termed it. Alternatively, we might be inclined at this point to give up and declare that this game is absurd. Perhaps we recognize that, yes, we have been caught in a structure of seeking a solution to a fabricated problem, but that now we can step outside it and see it for what it is. However, in making this move we simply slide into an unorthodox orientation and embrace the "discourse of immediacy."

UPGRADING FROM CHANGE TO IMMEDIACY

The problem with the discourse of change is that for as long as we take it seriously and try to live in terms of it, we will experience a lack or incompletion. Our meditation and other spiritual practices will be propelled by the belief that "This isn't it," and that there is still something to get. And whatever "it" we might achieve, or think we have achieved, there will always be more, there will always seem to be another, more authentic "it" further along the road, beckoning us to further change. And so the road stretches further and further ahead, and it looks as though we'll never reach the end of it; and maybe we're not on the right road anyway. This, of course, is what makes the perspective of immediacy look so attractive: if the problem is thinking that "This isn't it," then the solution is to get "This *is* it."

And so we decide to trade in our discourses of change for the "better" perspective of living fully in the present. In this new discourse we appreciate that "This is it," because it can't be anything else. We can't be doing one thing while we're doing another. We can't be thinking another thought when we are thinking the one that we are thinking now. While reading this sentence, we can't be reading another one. In this discourse, there is nothing to get, since we have already got whatever there is for us to get. The idea that one experience can displace another, or the suggestion there is something more to this experience, are simply constructs of the imagination. Similarly, the past and future are present-time constructs. Our memories are the present-time activation of images accompanied by the belief that these images represent real events that can't be happening now.

SEDUCED BY THE HERE AND NOW

While living in the here and now can seem attractive, if we think this perspective will be a solution to our problems, we should think again. First, living in the here and now is an illusion made real by the discourse of immediacy. There is actually no such thing as being totally in the present. If we are living in the here and now, by definition we can have no sense of being located in the present rather than the past or future. Thinking about tomorrow's work or recalling yesterday's conversation, neither displaces nor dilutes the quality of our experience since there is no qualitative difference between the thought of yesterday and today and tomorrow. If thinking about the past or future were less real than thinking about the present, we wouldn't take our memories and projections so seriously.

Second, in cultivating an experience of immediacy we fail to see how it becomes just another movement within the discourse of change. We misread traditions like Zen, and begin to think that this new perspective represents an improvement over our old ways of thinking and practicing. We think we are onto something good, a better bet. We believe that this new perspective is less constructed, truer to reality, or more liberating. Having escaped the limitation of needing to change, we end up right back where we began. The progress we seem to have made evaporates as we discover ourselves playing the same game of locating ourselves on a path leading to an ever more satisfying way of being.

And, in any case, why are we seduced by the proposition that the present is more authentic than the past or the future? Doesn't living entirely in the present seem to mean cutting off two thirds of our experience?

Thus, even though the perspective of immediacy isn't something that can be gained or avoided, we continue to regard it as an experience worth having. While the experience of immediacy is neither profound nor trivial, we think it is either super-profound or else ordinary in some very significant and generally inaccessible way. Even if we figure that immediacy is "nothing," we still want to get it. In this way, we continue to be trapped in a game of distinguishing our perspective as superior and advanced.

This illusion of progress can become compounded as we gain increased fluency in the rhetoric of immediacy. Even though immediacy isn't a knowledge- or skills-based perspective, we figure that we can learn it through exposure to the right teacher or course. We learn a new, "sophisticated" language that allows us to say that there is no difference between "having it" and "not having it," but we continue to approve and disapprove of different spiritual systems. We learn how to talk the talk, but it doesn't alleviate our basic discomfort and conflict.

Furthermore, we often take on board the idea of living in the moment only after we have struggled unsuccessfully to free ourselves from conflict and pain. We figure that if hard work has not delivered the goods, then we might as well give in to what is. We justify this shift by saying that suffering is caused by rejecting what we are experiencing. But to the extent that we are forced into "accepting the moment" through having failed to produce the changes we desire, this new perspective is stained by residual feelings of resignation and disappointment. "Living in the moment" can be a nice way of saying that we have run out of steam.

So while we may gain short-term relief from our suffering by thinking that we have made progress in entering the experience of immediacy, in time our conflict and dissatisfaction return as we struggle to cultivate and hang on to a preferred perspective.

• • •

Returning to the economic terms with which we started our discussion, in subscribing to the discourse of immediacy, we have declared that we believe no investment is necessary—enlightenment can be gained for no capital outlay at all. Or if we are a little more sophisticated, a little more familiar with the terms of this discourse, we might say that our problem is that the profit has already been made, the dividend has already been paid, and we actually have the check in our hands, but we're not sure where and how to cash it. Enlightenment is our natural condition, but we don't know how to make the transition from the theoretical to the real.

And so, just as the discourse of immediacy ultimately resolves itself into the discourse of change, so the economics of no-investment ultimately coils itself back into the economics of investment-and-return. We think we can do it without spending a cent, but we eventually find ourselves having to invest.

How can we escape the problem of automatically reconstructing the perspective of immediacy as simply another chapter within the discourse of change? Of course, it's not as simple as just saying that there is no problem, for this at once locates us within the rhetoric of immediacy, as a discourse that stands in contrast to the need to escape.

The more we talk about change and immediacy and explore their implications, the more we seem to become tangled in intractable paradox. The discourse of change seems inherently flawed, since it appears to rest on manifest fallacy, and the discourse of immediacy seems inherently impossible to apply, since it always appears to resolve itself into the discourse of change. We thought we were on firm and solid ground to begin with, but now we seem to be on a quicksand of contradiction, always poised on the edge of certainty.

It seems that the only alternative left is to be in a way where we are in neither discourse. Clearly, we need to get outside this whole thing of being trapped by language. We need to move into a space where we have neither "got it" nor "lost it." However, if we think of this as something worth getting, we fall back into the discourse of change. On the other hand, if we figure that this isn't something we can get, or that it is a meaningless state, we are trapped by the rhetoric of immediacy.

FALLING TO THE EXTREMES

If at this point we haven't given up entirely (or become unorthodox), then the problem that presents itself is how to be in a way that doesn't fall into either the orthodox or unorthodox extreme. However, as soon as we try to do this, we fall into the orthodox extreme of trying to do or not do something. On the other hand, if we just let things be as they are, without any concern for observing how we might fall into these extremes, we have fallen into the unorthodox extreme of letting go.

Perhaps our mistake is taking this notion of "falling to an extreme" too seriously. Perhaps there is no such thing as an extreme at all. We might declare that we are simply "thinking what we are thinking" when we think we are falling to an extreme. In other words, thinking that we are falling to an extreme isn't really falling to an extreme at all; it is just thinking that we are falling to an extreme. However, this is a position that stands in contrast to believing that we can fall to an extreme, and as a position, it falls to the unorthodox extreme of non-referentiality and meaninglessness.

So, whether we like it or not, it seems that we are left with the notion of falling to an extreme, that it actually means something. In fact, it begins to seem that all we can ever do is fall to an extreme. If we want to forge ahead, we fall to the orthodox extreme. If we decide to give up, we fall to the unorthodox extreme.

At this point, we might advocate a balanced or integrated approach that harmonizes both perspectives into a balanced way of life. However, in rejecting a dualistic approach in favor of an integrated perspective, what we have really done is create a new dualistic structure and re-enter the discourse of change. On the other hand, if we think there is no right or wrong way of understanding the spiritual endeavor, we lock ourselves into the discourse of immediacy. And if we think that it is preferable to be nonjudgmental, this judgment itself flings us right back into the discourse of change.

As soon as we distinguish a middle ground from the extremes, this becomes a new extreme, in the sense that the new options are that we are either in the middle or on the edge. We are either balanced or unbalanced, appropriate or inappropriate. To the extent that the middle ground is the place where we should be, therefore, it becomes a pole in another dualistic structure.

We might now be inclined to seek a resolution by boldly declaring that ultimately "there is nothing to do or not to do," or that we are "neither orthodox nor unorthodox." However, if we say this in a mood of "insight and understanding," we fall to the extreme of over-valuing what we are saying. We believe that the bi-negation really says something and that we know what this is. On the other hand, if we find that we are thrown into silence, or mouth the bi-negation "knowing" that it really doesn't say anything, we fall to the unorthodox extreme of meaninglessness and non-referentiality.

THE DILEMMA UNRESOLVED

Two observations seem appropriate in concluding. The first is that the question of when, how, and what would constitute finishing our journey together in my writing and your reading of this book only arises when we are positioned within an orthodox interpretation of the role of spiritual practice. If we feel dissatisfied and incomplete at this point, it at least provides an opportunity for us to appreciate that in this moment we are still fixated on goals and specific outcomes. On the other hand, if we are genuinely situated in the unorthodox framework then the question of "finishing" this book is totally irrelevant and nonsensical since there is nothing for us to show, resolve, demonstrate, or conclude!

Notes

INTRODUCTION

1. On the story of Marpa's payment for the teachings, see Chögyam Trungpa, *Cutting Through Spiritual Materialism* (Boston and London: Shambhala, 1987), pp. 33–37. For an account of Milarepa, see Lobsang Lhalungpa, *The Life of Milarepa* (Boston and London: Shambhala, 1985).

2. The story of the Buddha's extreme asceticism is given in the *Mahasihanada Sutta*, sutta no. 12, in the *Majjhima Nikaya* (see chapter 2, n. 2). An English translation can be found in Bhikkhu Nanamoli and Bhikkhu Bodhi, trans., *The Middle Length Discourses of the Buddha: A New Translation of the* Majjhima Nikaya (Boston: Wisdom Publications, 1995), pp. 164–178.

CHAPTER ONE

1. This is found in slightly different forms in more than one scripture, including the *Saccavibhanga Sutta* (no. 141 in the *Majjhima Nikaya*). See Bhikku Nanamoli and Bhikkhu Bodhi, trans., *The Middle Length Discourses of the Buddha: A New Translation of the* Majjhima Nikaya (Boston, MA: Wisdom Publications, 1995), pp. 1097–1101.

CHAPTER TWO

1. The term *Theravada* is used in this book as synonymous with *Nikaya* Buddhism (also known as *Hinayana*), that form of Buddhism which accepts only the Pali Canon as authoritative. While this definition represents various simplifications, the historical and doctrinal issues involved are not significant to the present purposes of this discussion.

2. The Pali Canon consists of three *pitakas* or collections (literally, "baskets"): the *Vinaya Pitaka*, which is largely concerned with the rules of monastic discipline; the *Sutta Pitaka*, which contains the suttas or discourses of the Buddha (and in some cases those of his enlightened disciples); and the *Abhidhamma Pitaka*, which gives an analytic account of the Buddha's teachings based on material found in the other two pitakas. In its written

form, the Pali Canon dates from around 80 B. C. E., having previously been transmitted orally. The only English translation of the entire canon is that of the Pali Text Society. However, there are numerous translations of particular sections of the canon, particularly the five *Nikayas* or sections of the *Sutta Pitaka*. These include Bhikku Nanamoli and Bhikkhu Bodhi, trans., *The Middle Length Discourses of the Buddha: A New Translation of the Majjhima Nikaya* (Boston: Wisdom Publications, 1995), and Maurice Walshe's translation of the *Digha Nikaya, Thus Have I Heard: The Long Discourses of the Buddha* (London: Wisdom, 1987); reprinted as *The Long Discourses of the Buddha: A Translation of the Digha Nikaya* (Boston: Wisdom, 1996).

3. Walshe, *Thus Have I Heard*, p. 435. (*Pasadika Sutta*, no. 29 in the *Digha Nikaya*). This description is found in numerous other places throughout the Pali Canon.

4. I do not refer here to "monks and nuns," for, strictly speaking, full monastic ordination for women is no longer possible in the Theravada tradition. The relevant vows must be administered by a given number of monks and nuns, and it has been impossible to fulfill these conditions in any Theravada country since the 11th century. Thus Theravada nuns are, properly speaking, novices (*samaneri*), who take only 10 vows as opposed to the 311 stipulated in the *Vinaya* for a fully ordained Theravada nun.

5. In fact, according to the Buddhist understanding of karma, while we can't exercise control over every aspect of our experience, we are still responsible for everything we experience, because there is no such thing as an "accident of nature," or "innocent victim"—these represent the ripening of selfish and misguided actions in previous lives.

6. Walshe, *Thus Have I Heard*, p. 132 (*Pasadika Sutta*, no. 29 in the *Digha Nikaya*).

7. See Ayya Khema, *Being Nobody, Going Nowhere* (Boston: Wisdom, 1987); Joseph Goldstein, *Insight Meditation* (Boston: Shambhala, 1993); Thich Nhat Hanh, *Present Moment, Wonderful Moment* (London: Rider Books, 1993), and his *The Miracle of Mindfulness* (London: Rider Books, 1991); Nyanaponika Thera, *The Heart of Buddhist Meditation* (London: Rider, 1962; York Beach, ME: Samuel Weiser, 1976).

8. Satipatthana-sutta (no. 10 in the *Majjhima Nikaya*). See Bhikku Nanamoli and Bhikku Bodhi, trans., *The Middle Length Discourses of the Buddha*, pp. 145–155.

9. Ayya Khema, *Being Nobody, Going Nowhere*, p. 16.

CHAPTER THREE

1. For a comprehensive treatment of the various schools of the Mahayana tradition see Paul Williams, *Mahayana Buddhism: The Doctrinal Formulations* (London: Routledge, 1989).

2. Edward Conze trans., *The Perfection of Wisdom in Eight Thousand Lines and Its Verse Summary* (Bolinas, CA: Four Seasons Foundation, 1973), p. 163.

The text speaks of "the vehicle of the Disciples and Pratyekabuddhas" (*Shravakayana* and *Pratyekabuddhayana*, respectively). The Mahayana says that in Nikaya or Hinayana Buddhism people can be liberated through hearing the dharma from others, or purely through their own resources. The former are called "listeners," or *shravakas*, and the latter are called the "independently awakened," or "Pratyekabuddhas."

3. Stephen Batchelor trans., *A Guide to the Bodhisattva's Way of Life* (Dharamsala: Library of Tibetan Works and Archives, 1979), p. 129.

4. D. T. Suzuki's translation in *Manual of Zen Buddhism* (London: Rider, 1950), p. 14.

5. See Robert Thurman, trans., *The Holy Teachings of Vimalakirti: A Mahayana Scripture* (University Park and London: Pennsylvania State University Press, 1976), p. 47.

6. A list of 10 perfecting disciplines is also found, the other four being skillful means (*upaya*), personal power (*bala*), resolution (*pranidana*), and a comprehensive knowledge (*jnana*) of all spiritual and psychological realities. For discussions of the perfecting disciplines, see Peter Fenner, *The Ontology of the Middle Way* (Dordrecht, Holland: Kluwer, 1991), pp. 209–302; and any of the various translations of Shantideva's *Bodhicharyavatara*, such as Stephen Batchelor, *A Guide to the Bodhisattva's Way of Life*; Kate Crosby and Andrew Skilton, *The Bodhicaryavatara* (Oxford and New York: Oxford University Press, 1996); B. Vesna and Alan Wallace, *A Guide to the Bodhisattva Way of Life (Bodhicaryavatara)* (Ithaca, NY: Snow Lion, 1997).

7. In common with many of the central figures in Buddhist history, the dates of some of these individuals are unknown or conjectural. Aryadeva is traditionally regarded as a disciple of Nagarjuna, but Nagarjuna's own dates are unknown beyond the likelihood that he lived during the fourth century C. E. Asanga may be placed during the fourth century, and Vasubhandu during the fourth or fifth. Vimalamitra's dates fall between the sixth and eighth centuries. Chandrakirti may be placed during the seventh century, and Shantideva during the seventh or eighth. Santarakshita and his disciple Haribhadra lived during the eighth century, as did Kamalashila. With Atisha and Naropa, we are on firmer ground: the former's life spans the years 982–1054; and the latter's 1016–1100.

8. For an account of the Buddhist monastic universities, see A.K. Warder, *Indian Buddhism*, 2nd ed., rev. (Delhi: Motilal Banarsidas, 1980), pp. 466–516.

9. The *Dashabhumika-sutra* (*Sutra on the Ten Grounds*), and the encyclopedic *Yogacharabhumi* (*Stages of Yogic Practice*) are the principal texts that lay out the bodhisattvas' path. (The *Dashabhumika-sutra* forms part of the compendious *Avatamsaka-sutra*, which is available in English translation by Thomas Cleary as *The Flower Adornment Sutra*). The *Bodhisattvabhumi* (the 15th volume of the later work) remains a standard textbook of the paths and stages in Mahayana monastic institutions. These graduated texts lay out the bodhisattva's development over a series of five paths (*panchamarga*) and ten

stages (*dashabhumi*). Madhyamaka renditions of the path, which are similarly based on the bodhisattva levels, are found in the *Madhyamakavatara* and *Bodhicharyavatara*.

10. Madhyamaka is traditionally divided into two types: the *Prasangika* or "Deconstructive" Madhyamaka and the *Svatantrika* or "Constructive" Madhyamaka. The first system is purely deconstructive whereas the Constructive Madhyamaka will, on occasions, establish a conceptual position using independent reasons and arguments. In this study, I am using the term "Madhyamaka" to refer only to the Deconstructionists.

11. The idea that Buddhism—or at least the enlightened viewpoint—is positionless can also be inferred from the Pali texts. The *Attakavagga Sutta*, for example, says that fixed opinions lie behind all attachment. This sutra also rejects that idea that the truth as such can be expressed in propositional form. See H. Saddhatissa's translation of the *Attakavagga Sutta* in *The Sutta-Nipata* (London: Curzon Press, 1985), pp. 91–113.

12. This term is often translated as "emptiness." However, emptiness or *shunyata* does not signify the absence of phenomena. Rather, it points to phenomena as open and lacking any substratum or core. It is thus essentially an extension of the *anatman* teaching of early Buddhism.

13. According to Madhyamaka, a state of liberation (*moksha*) or unconditional freedom (*nirvana*) can be gained only through the skillful and diligent use of paradoxical analysis (*prasanga-vichara*). Later Tibetan philosophers, and especially those of the Gelugpa school, incorporate this claim as a central tenet in their philosophical system. The founder of the Gelugpa school, Je Tsongkapa, for example, writes: "[A]nalytical meditation is necessary, since without practicing analytical meditation which cultivates the discriminating wisdom analysis of the import of selflessness, meditative realization will not emerge.... One seeks the understanding of selflessness repeatedly analyzing its meaning." (Robert A. F. Thurman, ed., *Life and Teachings of Tsong Khapa* [Dharamsala: Library of Tibetan Works and Archives, 1982], p. 114.)

It should be pointed out that the picture here is complicated by the fact that the Gelugpas distinguish between a conceptual and a non-conceptual insight into egolessness. This distinction, however, is used in a confusing way; it is the conceptual insight that is produced through logical analysis. This leaves us with the problem of how the conceptual insight is converted into a non-conceptual insight. Tsongkhapa seems to say that "inference is necessarily conceptual, but can with repeated meditational familiarization be brought to a level of non-conceptual experience." See Elizabeth Napper, *Dependent-Arising and Emptiness* (Boston: Wisdom Publications, 1989), p. 136. If analysis (equals inference) is a necessary factor in bringing the conceptual insight to the level of a non-conceptual insight, then the distinction in no way provides a solution to the problem we are addressing. If, on the other hand, analysis is immaterial to the conversion, we are squarely back with our original problem. Is the conversion causal or acausal?

A number of western scholars of Madhyamaka agree with the assessment that analysis produces insight. Frederick Streng (*Emptiness: A Study in Religious Meaning* [Nashville, TN: Abingdon Press, 1967], p. 156) writes: "dialectical activity is reality-being-realized." Robert A. F. Thurman (*Essence of True Eloquence: Reason and Enlightenment in the Central Philosophy of Tibet* [Princeton: Princeton University Press, 1983], p. 126) says: "Enlightenment as wisdom is perfected as the culmination of the most refined rational inquiry, not at the cost of reason."

14. Chandrakirti, *Madhyamakavatara* (*Introduction to the Middle Path*, English translation in *The Ontology of the Middle Way* by Peter Fenner [Dordrecht, Holland: Kluwer, 1991], 6.116–117. In his Commentary (*Bhashya*), 229–230, Chandrakirti adds that the disappearance of conceptuality comes about as a direct result of analysis, and that such dissipation of conceptuality is concomitant with the onset of insight into reality. Similarly, Shantideva, in his *Bodhicharyavatara* (see n. 6 to this chapter), claims that Madhyamaka analysis leads to liberation. In reply to a concern that analysis could get bogged down in an infinite regress with no natural conclusion, he writes that: "Once an object of investigation has been investigated, there is no basis for investigation. Since there is no basis [further analysis] does not arise, and that is called unconditional freedom (*nirvana*)" (9.111).

15. There are four major schools or orders within Tibetan Buddhism: Nyingma, Sakya, Kagyud, and Gelug. (Some recent scholars would amend the total to five, counting Bön as a heterodox form of Buddhism—cf. ch. 5, n. 14.) The Nyingma is the oldest of the Tibetan traditions deriving directly from India, and its origins can be traced to the First Transmission period (see ch. 5, n. 10). The central teaching of the Nyingma school is Dzogchen, which I discuss in chapter 5. The Sakya school was founded by Könchog Gyalpo (1034–1102), and was initially in many respects indistinguishable from the Nyingma. This school lays equal stress on the Mahayana and the Vajrayana teachings, and emphasizes a balance of scholarship and practice. The Kagyud school also emerged during the eleventh century, and is divided into various sub-schools. The Kagyud looks to four figures in particular as the founders of its lineage: Tilopa, Naropa, Marpa, and Milarepa. The highest teaching of this tradition is Mahamudra, briefly discussed in chapter 5. The Gelug, the most scholastic of the Tibetan schools, was founded as a reform movement by Tsongkapa (1357–1419), and lays great stress on the study and practice of Madhyamaka.

16. The reasoning behind these paradoxical arguments appears counterintuitive at first, because it conflicts with our commonsense way of thinking. This note provides the logic of the arguments, in order to convey a taste of Madhyamaka analyses. One may wish to find fault with the logic, but it is worth remembering that Madhyamaka meditators are primarily concerned with the pragmatics of deconstructing their attachment and aversion to who they are.

The following analysis explores the status of our self in terms of whether we are the same as, or different from, our body-mind. The analysis can also be performed in terms of whether we are "one or many."

The first option is that we are not the same as our body-mind, that we are different, in other words. According to Madhyamaka reasoning, if we are different from our body-mind, the person that we are either can be known or cannot be known. There are no other options. If we are not an object of knowledge, we cannot be known as something different from our body-mind, so this option collapses. The other option is that we are different from our body-mind and that this can be known.

Madhyamaka now reasons that if the non-psychic, non-physical self that we are is something that can be known (that is, discerned, or cognized), as it must be in order for it to be known as "different from the body-mind," then it can't be totally different from the body-mind because our body-mind defines the limits of knowledge, in the sense that whatever can be experienced is experienced in terms of the body-mind, specifically feelings, discriminations, and consciousness. If we are not our body-mind, yet we still wish to claim that we can be an object of knowledge, then we must be able to be known, located, and described, independently of and without reference to the body-mind. But this isn't possible and so we aren't different from our body-mind.

If we are truly different from our body-mind, then we are unrelated to our body-mind and hence cannot be known through any reference to the body-mind. The argument here is that the body-mind mediates all cognition through the sense and mental consciousnesses (*chitta-skandha*) and the body (*rupa-skandha*). Thus, if we are totally unrelated to our body-mind, we cannot be an object of knowledge—we can't know anything about ourselves. But given that we are talking about the self that we know ourselves to be, we cannot be intrinsically different from our body-mind. Thus, the position that we are different from our body-mind implies that we are our body-mind. The initial thesis implies its negation.

The second alternative is that we are the same as our body-mind. This is a negation of the preceding position. The refutation of this position hinges on whether we and our body-mind are individually distinguishable in the instance of their being the same thing. According to Madhyamaka reasoning they are either discernible or not. There are no other options.

If we and our body-mind are not distinguishable one from the other, as this position seems to imply, then we cannot say that we are the same as our body-mind, for this supposes that there are two things which are one: there may be our self, or our body-mind; but if both of them are in fact just one thing, then there can't be the two of them. This position collapses, because there is no such thing as a relationship in which something is related with, or to, itself; by definition, relationships require at least two things that can be differentiated. Thus, this interpretation of the relationship between our self and our body-mind describes something logically impossible.

It follows that when we use the term "we" or "I" and the phrase "our body-mind," we must be saying that they both refer to the same thing, but that somehow the single thing referred to can be distinguished as two different things. On this interpretation, however, the identity relationship is forsaken, for if things can be distinguished from each other in terms of their having different properties (such as being divisible in the case of the body-mind and indivisible into parts in the case of our self), then they are different. Thus, when a relationship is retained rather than forsaken as in the first interpretation, the position that we are the same as our body-mind, implies that they are different. Again the initial position entail its own negation. The only conclusion that can be drawn from this is that we are neither the same as, nor different from our body-mind.

17. See Nagarjuna, *Mulamadhyamakakarika* (*Principal Stanzas on the Middle Path*, English translation in Streng: *Emptiness: Study in Religious Meaning*), 10.14 and 22.1; and Chandrakirti, *Madhyamakavatara*, 6.121–165. For a detailed reconstruction of this analysis, see Peter Fenner, *The Ontology of the Middle Way*, pp. 54–73. A contemporary interpretation of Madhyamaka analysis appears in Peter Fenner, *Reasoning into Reality: A Systems–Cybernetics and Therapeutic Interpretation of Middle Path Analysis* (Boston: Wisdom Publications, 1994).

18. Shohei Ichimura, "A Study of the Madhyamika Method of Refutation and its Influence on Buddhist Logic," in *Journal of the International Association of Buddhist Studies* 4, no. 1 (1981): 92.

19. The Ch'an teachings are traditionally said to have originated in an episode in which the Buddha held up a flower before an assembly of his disciples and said nothing. No one understood the message except the monk Mahakasyapa. The Buddha then said, "I possess the true Dharma Eye, the Marvellous Mind of Nirvana, the True Form of the Formless, the Subtle Dharma Gate that does not rest on words and letters but is a special transmission outside of the scriptures. This I entrust to Mahakasyapa." (Hui-weng Wu-ming, *A Collection of Essential Material from the Zen Sect's Successive Records of the Lamp*, Book 1, quoted in Heinrich Dumoulin, *Zen Buddhism: A History*, vol. I [New York: Macmillan Publishing; London: Collier Macmillan Publishers, 1988], p. 9.)

20. Summarized from Philip Yampolsky, trans., *The Platform Sutra of the Sixth Patriarch* (New York: Columbia University Press, 1967), pp. 155–156 and D.T. Suzuki, *Essays in Zen Buddhism, First Series* (London: Rider, 1970), pp. 188-189.

21. Summarized from D. T. Suzuki, *Essays in Zen Buddhism*, pp. 189–190.

22. Yampolsky, *The Platform Sutra of the Sixth Patriarch*, p. 130.

23. Ibid., p. 132.

24. For a detailed account of Zen history, see Dumoulin, *Zen Buddhism: A History*.

25. *Hekiganroku*, Case 67 in K. Sekida, trans., *Two Zen Classics: Mumonkan and Hekiganroku* (New York and Tokyo: Weatherhill, 1977), pp. 326–328.

26. Suzuki, *Essays in Zen Buddhism,* First Series, p. 240.

27. *Mumonkan,* Case 7, in K. Sekida, *Two Zen Classics,* p. 44.

28. Hakuin, *Zazengi,* in K. Nishiyama and J. Stevens trans., *A Complete English Translation of Dogen Zenji's* Shobogenzo *(The Eye and Treasury of the True Law),* vol. I (Tokyo: Daihokkaikku Publishing, 1975), p. 40.

29. Hakuin, *Zazengi,* pp. 39–40.

30. See T. P. Kasulis, *Zen Action: Zen Person* (Honolulu: University of Hawaii Press, 1981), pp. 71–77.

31. For a fuller discussion of koans, see Isshu Miura and Ruth Fuller Sasaki, *The Zen Koan: Its History and Use in Rinzai Zen* (San Diego: Harcourt Brace Jovanovich, 1965) and their extended treatment of the same topic in *Zen Dust: The History of the Koan and Koan Study in Rinzai (Lin-Chi) Zen* (New York: Harcourt, Brace & World, 1966).

32. *Mumonkan,* Case 1. See Sekida, *Two Zen Classics: Mumonkan and Hekiganroku.* , p. 27 *ff.*

33. According to Philip Yampolsky (*Introduction to The Platform Sutra of the Sixth Patriarch,* p. 110, n. 63), the "original face" koan first appears in the *Koshoji* edition of the *Platform Sutra* and is not found in the earliest extant version, the *Tun Huang* text.

34. See Miura and Sasaki, *The Zen Koan,* p. 29.

35. Daisetz Suzuki, "Lectures on Zen Buddhism," in Eric Fromm et al., *Zen Buddhism and Psychoanalysis* (New York: Harper and Row, 1970), p. 50.

36. Richard de Martino, "The Human Situation and Zen Buddhism," in Fromm et al., *Zen Buddhism and Psychoanalysis,* p 161.

37. Ibid.

38. Ibid., p. 162.

39. Ibid., p. 163.

CHAPTER FOUR

1. On the history of Tantra, see N. N. Bhattacharyya, *History of the Tantric Religion* (New Delhi: Manohar, 1992). The question whether Hindu or Buddhist Tantra is the elder has fueled much (largely futile) controversy. Bhattacharyya does not espouse either view, but sees Tantra as a development of the Mother Goddess Cult, in origin neither Buddhist nor Hindu, but "a very ancient way of life, an undercurrent which influenced all forms of Indian religious systems in some way or another" (p. 223).

2. Chögyam Trungpa, *Cutting through Spiritual Materialism* (Boston and London: Shambhala, 1987), p. 234.

3. For further general discussion of Buddhist Tantra, see Tsong-ka-pa, *Tantra in Tibet: The Great Exposition of Secret Mantra,* Jeffrey Hopkins, trans. (London: George Allen & Unwin, 1997) and H. V. Guenther, *The Tantric View of Life* (Berkeley and London: Shambhala, 1972).

4. The transformation of emotional energy is also correlated with the Five *Jinas* (or "dhyani buddhas," as they are sometimes erroneously known), five "families" of buddhas, which are elucidated in the Yoga tantras: Vairochana,

Amitabha, Ratnasambhava, Amogasiddhi, and Akshobhya. Each Jina is associated with particular root emotional affliction and a corresponding aspect of enlightened wisdom:

JINA	WISDOM	AFFLICTION
Vairochana	Omnipresence	Ignorance
Amitabha	Even-minded	Pride
Ratnasambhava	Discriminating	Desire
Amogasiddhi	All-accomplishing	Jealousy
Akshobhya	Mirror-like	Anger

A Tantric practitioner has a natural affiliation with one or another of these Jinas, depending upon her or his emotional temperament and karmic propensity.

5. Quoted in Miranda Shaw, *Passionate Enlightenment: Women in Tantric Buddhism* (Princeton: Princeton University Press, 1994), p. 20.

6. See Tenzin Gyatso, Dalai Lama XIV, *Deity Yoga: In Action and Performance Tantra* (Ithaca, NY: Snow Lion, 1981), pp. 11–12.

7. Kelsang Gyatso, *Clear Light of Bliss: Mahamudra in Vajrayana Buddhism* (London: Wisdom Publications, 1982), p. 5.

8. David Snellgrove, *Indo-Tibetan Buddhism: Indian Buddhists and their Tibetan Successors,* 2 vols. (Boston: Shambhala, 1987), p. 278.

9. The term *yuganaddha* belongs to the father tantras, and derives from the *Guhyasamaja Tantra. Sahaja* is from the mother tantras.

10. Kennard Lipman, trans., *You Are the Eyes of the World* (Novato, CA: Lotsawa, 1987), p. 67.

11. On the *kriya* level, the deity is regarded as a master; on the *charya,* as a friend; on the *yoga,* as a sibling; and finally, on the *anuttarayoga* level, it is identified with oneself.

12. Lama Thubten Yeshe, *The Bliss of Inner Fire: Heart Practice of the Six Yogas of Naropa* (Boston: Wisdom Publications, 1998), p. 21.

13. Jamgon Kongtrul Lodrö Tayé, *Creation and Completion: Essential Points of Tantric Meditation* (Boston: Wisdom Publications, 1996), p. 36.

14. This is a subtle body composed of the vital energies or "winds" (*prana*) that circulate within an internal network of "psychic nerves" (*nadi*). This network consists primarily of a central channel (*avadhuti*), a left channel (*lalana*), and a right channel (*rasana*). These are surrounded by an intricate subsidiary system of nerves that branch out all over the body. ·

15. See Garma C. C. Chang, *The Six Yogas of Naropa and Teachings on Mahamudra* (Ithaca, NY: Snow Lion, 1977), for a (somewhat dated) presentation of these and other yogas. On Tibetan death and dying practices, see Robert A. F. Thurman, trans., *The Tibetan Book of the Dead: Liberation through Understanding in the Between* (New York: Bantam Books, 1994).

CHAPTER FIVE

1. Gampopa was criticized by other early Kagyud masters for delineating a

unique Mahamudra lineage. See David Jackson, *Enlightenment by a Single Means: Tibetan Controversies on the "Self-Sufficient White Remedy,"* (Vienna: Der Österreichischen Akadamie der Wissenschaften, 1994), pp. 55–58.

2. Sakya Pandita accused Ch'an, Dzogchen, and Mahamudra of teaching a flawed form of insight meditation (*vipashyana*) that led to an experience of "only openness," that is, an experience that cannot be integrated with the empirical reality of everyday appearances. According to the Sakya Pandita, the unorthodox approaches cause people to become fixated on openness as a vacuity, and so fail to lead to any real spiritual goal. See David Ruegg, *Buddha-nature, Mind and the Problem of Gradualism in a Comparative Perspective: On the Transmission and Reception of Buddhism in India and Tibet* (New Delhi: Heritage Publishers, 1992), p. 110.

3. Saraha's dates are unknown. However, scholars generally agree in placing him during the eighth or early ninth century C. E.

4. In the Kagyud tradition, this is known as the "Lineage of Mahamudra Realization." This lineage traces a direct line through the Indian *siddhas* Saraha, Nagarjuna, Savaripa, and Maitripa, to the Tibetan Marpa.

5. Chögyam Trungpa, et al., *The Life of Marpa the Translator by Tsang Nyon Heruka*, (Boston and London: Shambhala, 1986), p. 62.

6. Tashi Namgyal distinguishes this from "sutric" and "Tantric" Mahamudra, presenting it as a separate vehicle going back to Saraha. See Lobsang Lhalungpa, *Mahamudra: The Quintessence of Mind and Meditation by Takpo Tashi Namgyal* (Boston and London: Shambhala, 1986), p. 110.

7. According to David Germano, Dzogchen and Mahamudra probably stem from a largely active oral and nonmonastic movement that existed among circles of the Himalaya. See David Germano, "Architecture and Absence in the Secret Tantric History of the Great Perfection (rdzogs chen)," in *Journal of the International Association of Buddhist Studies* 17 no. 2 (1994):215–216.

8. Among the most significant Dzogchen texts is Garab Dorje's "Three Statements" (*tshig gsum*), which is available in English as John Reynolds, trans., *The Golden Letters* (Ithaca, NY: Snow Lion, 1996). The same work also contains some material on the history of Dzogchen. On Garab Dorje's dates, see n. 9 to this chapter.

9. These and certain other key figures in Buddhist history inhabit a realm on the borders between the historical and the legendary, whence it is difficult, and in some cases entirely impossible, to establish any precise biographical data. The difficulty is further compounded in certain instances by the same name being borne by more than one individual. Therefore, their dates can only be approximate. According to tradition, Mañjushrimitra was a disciple of Garab Dorje. Garab Dorje's dates are themselves conjectural, however; he is traditionally regarded as having lived during the first century C. E., but may have lived as much as two centuries later. Jnanasutra may be placed during either the third century C. E. or the sixth; Shrisimha and his disciple Vimalamitra may be placed between the sixth and eighth; and Vairochana

between the eighth and ninth. The figure of Padmasambhava is so set about with myth and legend that he becomes uniquely imponderable from the historical point of view (even leaving aside the eight manifestations under which he is known in Tantric practice and iconography). Tradition identifies him as the teacher and adoptive son of a certain king Indrabhuti, but there are at least three kings by that name—the one in question probably lived during the eighth or early ninth century C. E.

10. Buddhism reached Tibet by means of two "Transmissions" from India, in the course of which many Indian teachers and scholars travelled to Tibet, and virtually the entire corpus of Indian Buddhist literature was translated into Tibetan. The First Transmission covers the period from the seventh to ninth centuries, and is traditionally regarded as closing with the supposedly anti-Buddhist activities of the Tibetan King Lang Darma (ca. 803–842). The Second Transmission is traditionally dated from the time of the translator Rinchen Zangpo (959–1051).

11. See Tulku Thondup Rinpoche, *Buddha Mind: An Anthology of Longchen Rabjam's Writings on Dzogpa Chenpo*, Harold Talbott, ed. (Ithaca, N.Y.: Snow Lion, 1989), pp. 3–46. Tulku Thondup lays out the various divisions and classes within the Tantric system and identifies their distinctive practices and important texts.

12. Tsultrim Allione, *Women of Wisdom* (London: Routledge & Kegan Paul, 1984), p. 14.

13. This is hardly surprising, since Dzogchen emerged in the cross-cultural melting pot of northwestern India that also produced the Hindu Shaivite tradition. As Herbert Guenther has noted (*Wholeness Lost and Wholeness Regained*, p. 126, n. 63.), "Early rDzogs-chen thought evolved in areas where Gnostic ideas were rampant...." On Bön as a heterodox form of Buddhism, see Snellgrove, *Indo-Tibetan Buddhism*, pp. 390–391, 399 ff.

14. See Tenzin Wangyal, *Wonders of the Natural Mind: The Essence of Dzogchen in the Native Bön Tradition of Tibet* (Barrytown, NY: Station Hill Press, 1993) and Shardza Tashi Gyaltsen, *Heart Drops of Dharmakaya* (Ithaca, NY: Snow Lion, 1993), both of which are concerned with the Bön tradition of Dzogchen.

15. *Rang grol phyag rgya chen po*, fol. 162b.8–163a.6, Shaw's translation in *Passionate Enlightenment: Women in Tantric Buddhism*, p. 88. In the third line, Shaw has "reality" for *chos sku* (*dharmakaya*). I have substituted the term "dharmakaya."

16. Tsele Natsok Rangdröl, *Lamp of Mahamudra* (Boston and London: Shambhala, 1989), pp. 5–13.

17. Lobsang Lhalungpa, trans., *Mahamudra: The Quintessence of Mind and Meditation by Takpo Tashi Namgyal*. Boston and London: Shambhala, 1986, p. 245.

18. Nyanaponika Thera, trans., *Anguttara Nikaya*, I, 10 (Kandy, Sri Lanka: Buddhist Publication Society, 1981), p. 2.

19. Arya Maitreya and Acarya Asanga, *The Changeless Nature: Mahayana Uttara*

Tantra Sastra, Ken and Katia Holmes, trans. (Scotland: Karma Drubgyud Darjay Ling, 1979) 1:154–155:68.

20. Quoted in Tulku Thondup Rinpoche, *Buddha Mind*, p. 325.
21. Namkhai Norbu and Adriano Clemente, *The Supreme Source: The Kunjed Gyalpo, The Fundamental Tantra of Dzogchen Semde*, English trans. by Andrew Lukianowicz (Ithaca, NY: Snow Lion, 1999), pp. 67–68.
22. Cf. Lhalungpa, *Mahamudra*, p. 245.
23. David Stott, "The History and Teachings of the Early Dwags-po bKa' brgyud Tradition in India and Tibet," (Ph.D. diss., University of Manchester, England, 1985), pp. 125–126.
24. Longchenpa, (kLong chen rab 'byam pa), *The Natural Freedom of Being* (Gangtok, Sikkim: Dondrup Cehn Rinpoche, 1974), f. 67. The Tibetan title of this text is *Chos nyid rang grol.* It is one book in a trilogy titled *Rang grol skor gsum.* The first book in the trilogy titled *Sems nyid rang grol* has been translated twice: by Herbert V. Guenther as "The Natural Freedom of Mind," *Crystal Mirror* 4 (1975):113–146; and by Tulku Thondup Rinpoche as the "Naturally Liberated Mind" in *Buddha Mind*, pp. 316-354. I have been helped in translating the *Chos nyid rang grol* by David Christenson and Professor David Germano.
25. Namkhai Norbu, *Dzog chen and Zen* (Oakland, CA: Zhang Zhung Editions, 1984), p. 30.
26. Longchenpa, *The Natural Freedom of Being, f.* 68, 69.
27. Jamgon Kongtrul, *Creation and Completion*, p. 36.
28. Stott, "History and Teachings of the Early Dwags-po bKa' brgyud Tradition in India and Tibet," pp. 109–110.
29. Rangdröl, *Lamp of Mahamudra*, p. 17.
30. Namkhai Norbu, *Dzog chen and Zen*, p. 30.
31. Namkhai Norbu, *The Supreme Source*, pp. 112–113.

CHAPTER SIX

1. Notable among these is Maura "Soshin" O'Halloran, *Pure Heart, Enlightened Mind—The Zen Journal and Letters of Maura "Soshin" O'Halloran* (New York: Riverhead Books, 1995), which was compiled from letters and diary entries after her early death in a car accident.
2. The lives of the masters of the Mahamudra and Dzogchen traditions make very interesting reading, and provide another window on the unorthodox expressions of Buddhist enlightenment. Sample literature includes: David Templeman, trans., *The Seven Instruction Lineages of Jo Nang Taranatha* (Dharamsala: Library of Tibetan Works and Archives, 1983), *Taranatha's Life of Krsnacarya/Kanha* (Dharamsala: Library of Tibetan Works and Archives, 1989), and "Taranatha's Life of Kanha/Krsnacarya: an Unusual Siddha Hagiography," in *Tibetan Studies, Proceedings of the 5th Seminar of the International Association of Tibetan Studies*, Narita, 1992: 309-313; Keith Dowman, trans., *Masters of Enchantment: The Lives and Legends of the Mahasiddhas* (London: Arkana, 1988) and *Masters of Mahamudra: Songs and*

Histories of the Eighty-Four Buddhist Siddhas (Albany, NY: SUNY Press, 1985).

3. Quoted in Edward Conze, ed., *Buddhist Texts through the Ages* (New York: Harper & Row, 1954), p. 225.

4. Ibid., p. 226.

5. Quoted in Kamil V. Zvelebil, *The Poets of the Powers* (London: Rider, 1973), p. 100.

6. Longchenpa, *The Natural Freedom of Being*. See chapter 5, note 24.

7. Tibetan: *Rang sangs rgyas* (Sanskrit: *pratyekabuddha*)—one who has attained enlightenment without relying on a teacher.

8. Longchenpa, *The Natural Freedom of Being*, f. 61.

9. From the "Songs for the People" section of his *Collected Songs* (*Dohakosa*), translated by David Snellgrove in *Buddhist Texts through the Ages*, p. 227. For a translation and analysis of the "Songs for the King" see Herbert V. Guenther, *The Royal Song of Saraha* (Berkeley and London: Shambhala, 1973) and the same author's *Ecstatic Spontaneity: Saraha's Three Cycles of Doha* (Berkeley: Asian Humanities Press, 1993).

10. Thomas Cleary, trans., *Zen Essence: The Science of Freedom* (Boston: Shambhala, 1989), p. 1.

11. Ibid, p. 37.

12. Longchenpa, *The Natural Freedom of Being*, f. 63.

13. In earlier sections, he also refutes the methods of Buddhist tantra.

14. Longchenpa, *The Natural Freedom of Being*, f. 63.

15. Ibid.

16. Quoted in Conze, ed., *Buddhist Texts through the Ages*, p. 229.

17. Thomas Cleary, *Zen Essence*, p. 6.

18. Longchenpa, *The Natural Freedom of Being*, f. 63

19. Norman Waddell, trans. "The Zen Sermons of Bankei Yotaku," in *Eastern Buddhist* 6, no. 2 (1973): 147.

20. Norman Waddell, trans., "A Selection of Bankei's Zen Dialogues" in *Eastern Buddhist* 8 (1974): 114.

21. U. G. Krishnamurti is a non-aligned teacher who repudiates every label applied to him, as well as the suggestions that he is a teacher or has anything of spiritual worth to offer. In fact, he actively discourages people from listening to him, pointing out that such people are only interested in keeping their identities intact by getting more ideas to fuel their hopes for spiritual emancipation. While U. G. Krishnamurti is non-aligned, his upbringing was as a Hindu Brahmin. As a child, he was recognized as a yoga *bhrashta*—one who has come within inches of enlightenment in his previous life. In his early years, he diligently practiced all forms of yoga and gained the full range of *samadhi* experiences that the texts describe. In his forty-ninth year, he had an experience that he refers to as "the calamity," in which the questions about enlightenment and any concerns for this state totally disappeared. In *The Mystique of Enlightenment: The Unrational Idea of a Man called U.G.* (Goa, India: Dinesh Vaghela Cemetile, 1982), p. 19, he reports: "Then suddenly the question disap-

peared. Nothing happened; the question just disappeared. I didn't say to myself 'Oh, my God! Now I have found the answer.' Even that state disappeared. The whole thing is finished for me, and that's all, you see. From then on, never did I say to myself, 'Now I have the answer to all those questions.' That state of which I had said, 'This is the state'—that state disappeared. The question disappeared. Finished, you see. It is not emptiness, it is not blankness, it is not the void, it is not any of those things; the question disappears suddenly, and that is all."

22. Krishnamurti, *The Mystique of Enlightenment*, p. 62.

23. Ibid., pp. 95, 149.

24. The mind-nature is popularly referred to as "no mind" (*wu-hsin*) in Ch'an texts. This is the same as the Ch'an notion of "non-thought" (*wu-nien*). In the *Platform Sutra* (*T'an ching*), non-thought signifies a detached engagement with whatever arises in one's experience, such that thought can be active yet not condition the mind. See Yampolsky, *The Platform Sutra of the Sixth Patriarch*, p. 153.

25. Ho tse Shen-hui was not, however, the first Chinese teacher to introduce the notion of sudden awakening. The Chinese scholar Tao-Sheng (360–434) advocated a sudden awakening theory in a short-lived movement that was absorbed into the T'ien-t'ai philosophy. See Dumoulin, *Zen Buddhism*, p. 77 and Carl Bielefeldt, *Dogen's Manual of Zen Meditation* (Berkeley: University of California Press, 1988), p. 87.

26. John McRae, "The Ox-head School of Chinese Ch'an Buddhism: From Early Ch'an to the Golden Age," in Gimello and Gregory, eds., *Studies in Ch'an and Hua-Yen* (Honolulu: University of Hawaii Press, 1983), pp. 169–252.

27. Yampolsky, *The Platform Sutra*, p. 148.

28. See Robert Buswell, *The Korean Approach to Zen: The Collected Works of Chinul* (Honolulu, University of Hawaii Press, 1983), pp. 43–45.

29. From Chinul's *Excerpts from the Dharma Collection and Special Practice Record*, ibid., 267.

30. Longchenpa, *The Natural Freedom of Being*, f. 64.

31. Conze, ed., *Buddhist Texts through the Ages*, p. 226.

32. Thomas Cleary, *Zen Essence*, p. 78.

33. Ibid., p. 69.

34. H. W. L. Poonja, *Wake Up and Roar* (Kula, Hawaii: Pacific Center Pub., 1992), p. 66.

35. Longchenpa, *The Natural Freedom of Being*, f. 64

36. Ibid. *f.* 66.

37. Ibid.

38. Poonja, *Wake Up and Roar*, p. 117.

39. Longchenpa, *The Natural Freedom of Being*, ff. 66-67.

40. Ibid. *f.* 67

41. John Reynolds, trans., *The Golden Letters*, p. 149.

42. Thomas Cleary, *Zen Essence*, p. 44.

43. Longchenpa, *The Natural Freedom of Being, f.* 67.
44. Ibid. *f.* 68.
45. This metaphor is also used by Saraha. See David Templeman, "Doha, Vajragiti and Carya Songs," in G. Samuel, H. Gregor, and E. Stutchbury, eds., *Tantra and Popular Religion in Tibet* (New Delhi: Aditya Prakashan, 1987), p. 29.
46. Longchenpa, *The Natural Freedom of Being, f.* 68.

CHAPTER SEVEN

1. There is nothing to be gained in trying to trace these back to Madhyamaka or Dzogchen, since both traditions advocate most of these attitudes at one time or another.
2. Chokyi Nyima Rinpoche, *The Union of Mahamudra and Dzogchen,* Eric Pema Kunsang, trans. (Hong Kong: Rangjung Yeshe Publications, 1989), p. 187. See also Kalu Rinpoche, *Luminous Mind: The Way of the Buddha* (Boston: Wisdom Publications, 1997), pp. 229–230.
3. Yampolsky, *The Platform Sutra of the Sixth Patriarch,* p. 137.
4. Thomas Cleary, *Zen Essence,* p. 77.
5. The construct of "two truths or realities" (*satyadvaya*) dates back to Nagarjuna, and is regarded as one of his greatest contributions to Buddhist theory. This formulation helps to explain the relationship between the phenomenal world and openness, and attempts to harmonize the paradox presented in the Prajnaparamita sutras, which proclaim both the existence and nonexistence of a path.
6. Mañjushrimitra, *Primordial Experience: An Introduction to rDzogs-chen Meditation,* Namkhai Norbu and Kennard Lipman, trans. (Boston and London: Shambhala, 1987), p. 61.

Bibliography

Allione, Tsultrim. *Women of Wisdom*. London: Routledge & Kegan Paul, 1984.

Batchelor, Stephen, trans. *A Guide to the Bodhisattva's Way of Life*. Dharamsala: Library of Tibetan Works and Archives, 1979.

Bhattacharyya, N. N. *History of the Tantric Religion*. New Delhi: Manohar, 1992.

Bielefeldt, Carl. *Dogen's Manual of Zen Meditation*. Berkeley: University of California Press, 1988.

Broido, Michael. "Padma dKar-po on Tantra as Ground, Path and Goal." *The Journal of the Tibet Society* 5 (1985): 5-54.

Buswell, Robert. Jr. *The Korean Approach to Zen: The Collected Works of Chinul*. Honolulu: University of Hawaii Press, 1983.

Chandrakirti. *Madhyamakavatarabhasyya*. Tibetan text in *Madhyamakavatara par Candrakirti* by Louis de la Vallée Poussin. Reprint, Osnabruck, Germany: Biblio Verlag, 1970.

————. *Madhyamakavatara*. English translation in *The Ontology of the Middle Way* by Peter Fenner. Dordrecht, Holland: Kluwer Publishing, 1991.

Chang, Garma C. C. *The Six Yogas of Naropa and Teachings on Mahamudra*. Ithaca, NY: Snow Lion, 1977. Originally published as *Teachings of Tibetan Yoga*, New Hyde Park, NY: University Books, 1963.

Chokyi Nyima, Rinpoche. *The Union of Mahamudra and Dzogchen.* Trans. Eric Pema Kunsang. Hong Kong: Rangjung Yeshe Publications, 1989.

Cleary, Thomas, trans. *The Flower Adornment Sutra.* 3 vols. Boston and London: Shambhala, 1985.

———. *Rational Zen: The Mind of Dogen Zenji.* Boston: Shambhala, 1992.

———. *Shobogenzo: Zen Essays by Dogen.* Honolulu: University of Hawaii Press, 1986.

———. *Zen Dawn: Early Zen Texts from Tun Huang.* Boston: Shambhala, 1986.

———. *Zen Essence: The Science of Freedom.* Boston: Shambhala, 1989.

Conze, Edward, ed. *Buddhist Texts through the Ages.* New York: Harper & Row, 1954.

———, trans. *The Perfection of Wisdom in Eight Thousand Lines and Its Verse Summary.* Bolinas, CA: Four Seasons Foundation, 1973.

Crosby, Kate and Andrew Skilton, trans., *The Bodhicaryavatara.* Oxford and New York: Oxford University Press, 1996.

Dalai Lama. *A Flash of Lightning in the Dark of Night: A Guide to the Bodhisattva's Way of Life.* Boston: Shambhala, 1994.

De Martino, Richard. "The Human Situation and Zen Buddhism." In Eric Fromm, et al., *Zen Buddhism and Psychoanalysis.* New York: Harper and Row, 1970.

Dogen. *A Primer of Soto Zen: A Translation of Dogen's Shobogenzo Zuimonki.* Trans. Reiho Masunaga. Honolulu: University of Hawaii Press, 1971.

Dowman, Keith. *Masters of Enchantment: The Lives and Legends of the Mahasiddhas.* London: Arkana, 1988.

———, trans. *Masters of Mahamudra: Songs and Histories of the Eighty-Four Buddhist Siddhas.* Albany: State University of New York Press, 1985.

Dumoulin, Heinrich. *Zen Buddhism: A History.* 2 vols. New York: Macmillan Publishing; London: Collier Macmillan Publishers, 1988.

Fenner, Peter. "Existential Psychology and the Complete Fulfillment (rDzogs chen) Tradition." *Journal of Contemplative Psychology* 9 (1994).

———. *The Ontology of the Middle Way.* Dordrecht, Holland: Kluwer Publishing, 1991.

———. *Reasoning into Reality: A Systems-Cybernetics and Therapeutic Interpretation of Middle Path Analysis.* Boston: Wisdom Publications, 1994.

Fenner, Peter and Penny Fenner. *Essential Wisdom Teachings: The Way to Inner Peace.* York Beach, ME: Nicolas-Hays, 2001.

Garfield, Jay L. *The Fundamental Wisdom of the Middle Way: Nagarjuna's* Mulamadhyamakakarika. New York: Oxford University Press, 1995.

Germano, David. "Architecture and Absence in the Secret Tantric History of the Great Perfection (rdzogs chen)." In *Journal of the International Association of Buddhist Studies* 17 no. 2 (1994): 203-335.

Goldstein, Joseph. *Insight Meditation: The Practice of Freedom.* Boston: Shambhala Publications, 1993.

Gómez, Luis O. "Indian Materials on the Doctrine of Sudden Enlightenment." In *Early Ch'an in China and Tibet.* Edited by Whalen Lai and Lewis R. Lancaster. Berkeley: Asian Humanities Press, 1983.

Guenther, Herbert V. *Kindly Bent to Ease Us.* 3 vols. Emeryville, CA: Dharma Publishing, 1976.

———. "The Natural Freedom of Mind." *Crystal Mirror* 4 (1975): 113–146.

———. *The Royal Song of Saraha: A Study in the History of Buddhist Thought.* Berkeley and London: Shambhala, 1973.

———. *The Tantric View of Life.* Berkeley and London: Shambhala, 1972.

———. *Wholeness Lost and Wholeness Regained: Forgotten Tales of Individuation from Ancient Tibet.* Albany: State University of New York Press, 1994.

———. trans. *Ecstatic Spontaneity: Saraha's Three Cycles of Doha.* Berkeley: Asian Humanities Press, 1993.

Gyaltsen, Shardza Tashi. *Heart Drops of Dharmakaya*. Ithaca, NY: Snow Lion Publications, 1993.

Hanh, Thich Nhat. *The Miracle of Mindfulness: A Manual on Meditation*. London: Rider Books, 1991.

———. *Present Moment, Wonderful Moment*. London: Rider Books, 1993.

Ichimura, Shohei. "A Study of the Madhyamika Method of Refutation and Its Influence on Buddhist Logic." *Journal of the International Association of Buddhist Studies* 4 no. 1 (1981): 87–95.

Jackson, David. *Enlightenment by a Single Means: Tibetan Controversies on the "Self-Sufficient White Remedy."* Vienna: Der Österreichischen Akadamie der Wissenschaften, 1994.

Jamgon Kongtrul Lodrö Tayé. *Creation and Completion: Essential Points of Tantric Meditation*. Translation, annotation, and introduction by Sarah Harding. Boston: Wisdom Publications, 1996.

Kalu Rinpoche. *Luminous Mind: The Way of the Buddha*. Boston: Wisdom Publications, 1997.

Kasulis, T. P. *Zen Action: Zen Person*. Honolulu: University of Hawaii Press, 1981.

Kelsang Gyatso. *Clear Light of Bliss: Mahamudra in Vajrayana Buddhism*. London: Wisdom Publications, 1982.

Kenchen Thrangu, Rinpoche. *The Ornament of Clear Realization: Asanga's Commentary on the Prajnaparamita*. Translated by Ken and Katia Holmes. Boulder: Namo Buddha Seminar, 1994.

Khema, Ayya. *Being Nobody, Going Nowhere*. Boston: Wisdom Publications, 1987.

Krishnamurti, U. G. *The Mystique of Enlightenment: The Unrational Idea of a Man called U. G.* Edited by Rodney Arms. Goa, India: Dinesh Vaghela Cemetile Co., 1982.

Lhalungpa, Lobsang. *The Life of Milarepa*. Boston and London: Shambhala, 1985.

————, trans. *Mahamudra: The Quintessence of Mind and Meditation by Takpo Tashi Namgyal.* Boston and London: Shambhala, 1986.

Lipman, Kennard, trans. *You Are the Eyes of the World.* Novato, CA: Lotsawa, 1987.

Longchenpa (kLong chen rab 'byam pa). *The Natural Freedom of Being* (Rang grol skor gsum). Gangtok, Sikkim: Dodrup Chen Rinpoche, 1974.

McRae, John R. "The Ox-head School of Chinese Ch'an Buddhism: From Early Ch'an to the Golden Age." In *Studies in Ch'an and Hua-Yen.* Edited by Robert M. Gimello and Peter N. Gregory. Honolulu: University of Hawaii Press, 1983.

Maitreya, Arya and Acarya Asanga. *The Changeless Nature: Mahayana Uttara Tantra Sastra.* Translated by Ken and Katia Holmes. Scotland: Karma Drubgyud Darjay Ling, 1979.

Mañjushrimitra. *Primordial Experience: An Introduction to rDzogs-chen Meditation.* Translated by Namkhai Norbu and Kennard Lipman. Boston and London: Shambhala, 1987.

Miura, Isshu and Ruth F. Sasaki. *Zen Dust: The History of the Koan and Koan Study in Rinzai (Lin-Chi) Zen.* New York: Harcourt, Brace & World, 1966.

————. *The Zen Koan: Its History and Use in Rinzai Zen.* San Diego: Harcourt, Brace & World, 1965.

Nagarjuna. *Mulamadhyamakakarika.* English translation in *Emptiness: Study in Religious Meaning* by Frederick J. Streng. Nashville, TN: Abingdon Press, 1967.

Napper, Elizabeth. *Dependent-Arising and Emptiness.* Boston: Wisdom Publications, 1989.

Nishiyama, K. and J. Stevens, trans. *A Complete English Translation of Dogen Zenji's* Shobogenzo *(The Eye and Treasury of the True Law).* 2 vols. Tokyo: Daihokkaikku Publishing Company, 1975.

Norbu, Namkhai. *The Cycle of Day and Night: Where One Proceeds Along the Path of Primordial Yoga.* Translated and edited by John Reynolds. Oakland, CA: Zhang Zhung Editions, 1984.

———. *Dzog chen and Zen.* Oakland, CA: Zhang Zhung Editions, 1984.

Norbu, Namkhai and Adriano Clemente. *The Supreme Source: The Kunjed Gyalpo, The Fundamental Tantra of Dzogchen Semde.* English translation from Italian by Andrew Lukianowicz. Ithaca, NY: Snow Lion Publications, 1999.

Nyanaponika Thera. *The Heart of Buddhist Meditation: A Handbook of Mental Training Based on the Buddha's Way of Mindfulness.* London: Rider, 1962; York Beach, ME: Samuel Weiser, 1976.

———. trans. *Anguttara Nikaya: Discourses of the Buddha.* 3 vols. Kandy, Sri Lanka: Buddhist Publication Society, 1981.

Nyima, Chokyi Rinpoche. *The Union of Mahamudra and Dzogchen.* Translated by Erik Pema Kunsang. Hong Kong: Rangjung Yeshe Publications, 1995.

O'Halloran, Maura "Soshin." *Pure Heart, Enlightened Mind—The Zen Journal and Letters of Maura "Soshin" O'Halloran.* Boston: Tuttle Publishing, 1994.

Poonja, H. W. L. *Wake Up and Roar.* Kula, Hawaii: Pacific Center Pub., 1992.

Rahula, Walpola S. *What the Buddha Taught.* New York: Grove Press, 1974.

Rangdröl, Tsele Natsok. *Lamp of Mahamudra.* Translated by Erik Pema Kunsang. Boston and London: Shambhala, 1989.

Reynolds, John M., trans. *The Golden Letters.* Ithaca, NY: Snow Lion Publications, 1996.

Ruegg, David Seyfort. *Buddha-nature, Mind and the Problem of Gradualism in a Comparative Perspective: On the Transmission and Reception of Buddhism in India and Tibet.* London: School of Oriental and African Studies, 1989; Reprint, New Delhi: Heritage Publishers, 1992.

Saddhatissa, H. trans. *The Sutta-Nipata.* London: Curzon Press, 1985.

Sekida, K., trans. *Two Zen Classics: Mumonkan and Hekiganroku.* New York and Tokyo: Weatherhill, 1977.

Shantideva. *Bodhicaryavatara.* English translation of chapter nine by M. J. Sweet in "Santideva and the Madhyamika: The Prajnaparamita-pariccheda of the *Bodhicaryavatara.*" Ph.D. diss., University of Wisconsin-Madison, 1972.

————. *Bodhicaryavatara.* English translation of chapter nine with commentary of H. H. the Dalai Lama by B. Alan Wallace in *Transcendent Wisdom: A Commentary on the Ninth Chapter of Shantideva's Guide to the Bodhisattva Way of Life.* Ithaca, NY: Snow Lion, 1988.

Shaw, Miranda. *Passionate Enlightenment: Women in Tantric Buddhism.* Princeton: Princeton University Press, 1994.

Snellgrove, David. *Indo-Tibetan Buddhism: Indian Buddhists and Their Tibetan Successors.* 2 vols. Boston: Shambhala, 1987.

Stott, David J. *The History and Teachings of the Early Dwags-po bKa' brgyud Tradition in India and Tibet.* Ph.D. diss., University of Manchester, England, 1985.

Streng, Frederick J. *Emptiness: A Study in Religious Meaning.* Nashville, TN: Abingdon Press, 1967.

Suzuki, Daisetz T. *Essays in Zen Buddhism, First Series.* London: Rider and Co., 1970.

————. "Lectures on Zen Buddhism." In Eric Fromm, et al. *Zen Buddhism and Psychoanalysis.* New York: Harper and Row, 1970.

————. *Manual of Zen Buddhism.* London: Rider, 1950.

Templeman, David, trans. *The Seven Instruction Lineages of Jo Nang Taranatha.* Dharamsala: Library of Tibetan Works and Archives, 1983.

————. *Taranatha's Life of Krsnacarya/Kanha.* Dharamsala: Library of Tibetan Works and Archives, 1989.

————. "Taranatha's Life of Kanha/Krsnacarya—An Unusual Siddha Hagiography." In *Tibetan Studies, Proceedings of the 5th Seminar of the International Association of Tibetan Studies,* Narita, 1992: 309–313.

————. "Doha, Vajragiti and Carya Songs." *Tantra and Popular Religion in Tibet.* Edited by G. Samuel, H. Gregor, and E. Stutchbury. New Delhi: Aditya Prakashan, 1987.

Tenzin Gyatso, Dalai Lama XIV. *Deity Yoga: In Action and Performance Tantra.* Ithaca, NY: Snow Lion, 1981.

Thondup Rinpoche, Tulku. *Buddha Mind: An Anthology of Longchen Rabjam's Writings on Dzogpa Chenpo.* Edited by Harold Talbott. Ithaca, N.Y.: Snow Lion, 1989.

Thurman, Robert A. F. *Essence of True Eloquence: Reason and Enlightenment in the Central Philosophy of Tibet.* Princeton: Princeton University Press, 1983.

————. *The Tibetan Book of the Dead: Liberation through Understanding in the Between.* New York: Bantam Books, 1994.

————. *Inside Tibetan Buddhism: Ritual and Symbols Revealed.* San Francisco: Collins Publisher San Francisco, 1995.

————, ed. *Life and Teachings of Tsong Khapa.* Dharamsala: Library of Tibetan Works and Archives, 1982.

————, trans. *The Holy Teachings of Vimalakirti: A Mahayana Scripture.* University Park and London: Pennsylvania State University Press, 1976.

Trungpa, Chögyam. *Cutting Through Spiritual Materialism.* Boston and London: Shambhala, 1987.

Trungpa, Chögyam, with Nalanda Translation Committee, trans. *The Life of Marpa the Translator by Tsang Nyon Heruka.* Boston and London: Shambhala, 1986.

Tsong ka pa. *Tantra in Tibet: The Great Exposition of Secret Mantra.* Translated by Jeffrey Hopkins. London: George Allen & Unwin, 1997.

Vesna, B. and Alan Wallace. *A Guide to the Bodhisattva Way of Life* (Bodhicaryavatara). Ithaca, NY: Snow Lion, 1997.

Waddell, Norman. "A Selection of Bankei's Zen Dialogues." *Eastern Buddhist* 8 (1974).

————. trans. "The Zen Sermons of Bankei Yotaku." *Eastern Buddhist* 6 no. 2 (1973).

Walshe, Maurice, trans. *Thus Have I Heard: The Long Discourses of the Buddha.* London: Wisdom Publications, 1987.

Wangyal, Tenzin. *Wonders of the Natural Mind: The Essence of Dzogchen in the Native Bön Tradition of Tibet.* Barrytown, NY: Station Hill Press, 1993.

Warder, A. K. *Indian Buddhism.* 2nd ed., rev. Delhi: Motilal Banarsidass, 1980

Williams, Paul. *Mahayana Buddhism: The Doctrinal Formulations.* London: Routledge, 1989.

Yampolsky, Philip B., trans. *The Platform Sutra of the Sixth Patriarch.* New York: Columbia University Press, 1967.

Yeshe, Lama Thubten. *The Bliss of Inner Fire: Heart Practice of the Six Yogas of Naropa.* Boston: Wisdom Publications, 1998.

———. *Introduction to Tantra: A Vision of Totality.* Ed. Jonathan Landaw. Boston: Wisdom Publications, 1987.

Zangpo, Ngawang, trans. *Jamgon Kongtrul's Retreat Manual.* Ithaca, NY: Snow Lion, 1994.

Zvelebil, Kamil V. *The Poets of the Powers.* London: Rider & Co., 1973.

Index